The Singing Web

Books by Mary Summer Rain

Nonfiction

Spirit Song
Phoenix Rising
Dreamwalker
Phantoms Afoot
Earthway
Daybreak
Soul Sounds
Whispered Wisdom
Ancient Echoes
Bittersweet
Mary Summer Rain's Guide to Dream Symbols
The Visitation
Millennium Memories
Fireside
Eclipse
The Singing Web

Fiction

The Seventh Mesa

Children's

Mountains, Meadows and Moonbeams
Starbabies

Books on Tape

Spirit Song
Phoenix Rising
Dreamwalker
Phantoms Afoot
The Visitation

The Singing Web

Mary Summer Rain

Cover design by Grace Pedalino

For information write:

Hampton Roads Publishing Company, Inc.
134 Burgess Lane
Charlottesville, VA 22902

Or call: 804-296-2772
FAX: 804-296-5096
e-mail: hrpc@hrpub.com
Web site: http://www.hrpub.com

If you are unable to order this book from your local bookseller, you may order directly from the publisher. Quantity discounts for organizations are available. Call 1-800-766-8009, toll-free.

Library of Congress Catalog Card Number: 99-71624

ISBN 1-57174-141-0

10 9 8 7 6 5 4 3 2 1

Printed on acid-free paper in the United States

Dedication

To Cheyenne

For the love and comfort you provided when no one else was there. Though you're gone, you'll always be in my heart.

TABLE OF CONTENTS

FOREWORD ~ 9

SECTION I: GRANDMOTHER'S GIFTS OF LIFE

Riches from the Depths of Her Heart ~ 13

Gemstones ~ 15

Rocks ~ 42

Metals ~ 58

Beauty from Her Opened Hands ~ 67

Flowers ~ 69

Trees ~ 91

Life from Her Whispered Breath ~ 117

People of the Earth ~ 119

People of the Air ~ 150

People of the Waters ~ 173

SECTION II: GRANDMOTHER'S GIFTS OF SPIRIT

Gifts from Her Spirit ~ 201

Wisdom, Intuition, and Dreams ~ 202

Foreword

From ancient nature beliefs to recent discoveries of modern day physicists, the reality of life's luminous interconnectedness through influencing energies has verified the fact that all of life is related, that the separate beingness of every living cell in the world is inexplicably interwoven into a singular pattern of wholeness, now recognized as the Great Web of Life. We are each a unique vibration upon that Web—sensitive and highly responsive to the finest vibratory movements of all other life forms existing upon its shimmering strands. And nowhere is this more evident than within nature—within Grandmother Earth's bountiful beingness. Indeed, we and nature are each as a strand of life's fragile DNA web that literally sings with the vibrating Song of Life.

The idea for the *The Singing Web* came from each one of you who wrote to ask questions about the influences of differing vibrational energies in physical reality. The idea came from your questions about the unique energies of specific animals and the inherent influences which can emanate from them. Inquiries regarding the energy empowerment of precious gems, metals, and common rocks found during a hike revealed your desire for me to share my perception of these qualities gifted from Grandmother Earth's many facets. You asked about the influences that certain trees and flowers had upon the human body, mind, and spirit—specific flowers not covered in aromatherapy literature. You sent in hundreds of questions which, in turn, gave me hundreds of issues to address. My readers were asking for information on the various aspects of nature which had the power to affect humankind in a multitude of ways. What you asked for was information on nature's vibrationary "influences." In an attempt to satisfy that need, I give you *The Singing Web*—Blessings from Grandmother Earth.

I've separated Grandmother's physical gifts from Her spiritual ones. In each section I've listed the nature elements you've been inquiring about and given the "general dream symbology" and the "specific influencing energy" characteristic for each. At the end of each section I've included responses to actual readers' questions regarding these. Incorporating these questions in the book gives the general public an opportunity to gain expanded knowledge and increased information generated from the questions of others. I've found that a specific question from one reader will represent at least a hundred others wondering about the same thing. You, the readers, have inspired this book. Because it has always been my intention to address as many of your questions as possible and provide simple and clear answers to them, your encouragement for me to create this unique volume has been responded to enthusiastically.

SECTION I

Grandmother's Gifts of Life

Riches from the Depths of Her Heart

Since the time of the ancients, perceptive people in a multitude of cultures have recognized and valued the powerful influences of gems, rocks, and metals unearthed while digging out the tunneled corridors beneath the foundations of their temples and pyramids. Not only were these natural elements valued for their obvious external beauty, but also for the subtle yet powerful influences felt from them. Thereafter, these bounties from the earth became integrated into the people's healing methodology, religious rituals, ceremonies of state, and were used for inspirational and developmental purposes. From coronation to divination, used by princess and pauper alike, these gifts of nature were perceived as being powerful and essential tools for daily living. Today the quality and strength of their influence has not waned with the passing of time. With the dawn of this current era's millennium, Grandmother Earth remains as vitally alive and fertile as ever. She is the Nature Goddess, our provider. Her essence can be found humming and singing from every strand on life's pulsating web. She is the nurturing force of life. Since the beginning of time, every culture had a name for the Goddess who symbolized Earth and her bounties. Though her ancient name is Gaea, she is most often recognized by the people of every land and nation as the selfless and eternally wise—Grandmother. With deepest respect, I now address the riches from the depths of her heart.

A note about this section: Gemologists, petrologists, and mineralogists will frequently intermix these three unique elements of the earth. Specialized technical books on gemology will include minerals (metals) and rocks. The same happens with technical mineral books which include gems. I found the line separating these to be a fine one; extremely subtle, often indistinct. Some elements can be appropriate for more than one category, therefore; I have come to the same conclusion when attempting to differentiate between some of them. For the purpose of this book, I've categorized them according to the common perception of the general public.

GEMSTONES

Achronite

Symbology: an ability capable of multiple utilizations

Influencing energy: inspires knowledge of opportunities to use one's talents

Alabaster

Symbology: emotional hardness; cold and indifferent attitude

Influencing energy: reinforces perspective of indifference

Alexandrite

Symbology: mood fluctuations

Influencing energy: assists in emotional stabilization

Almandine

Symbology: melancholia

Influencing energy: mood enhancer; uplifts perspective

Amber

Symbology: resiliency; loyalty

Influencing energy: augments a sense of assuredness

Amethyst

Symbology: vibrational element; dream aspects; spiritual inner beauty which shines through to the without

Influencing energy: raises vibrations; enhances dream memory

Amazonite

Symbology: a healing element in one's life

Influencing energy: works to improve more serious health problems

Andalusite

Symbology: depression

Influencing energy: improves perspectives regarding one's personal affairs; raises general outlook on life

Anglesite
Symbology: mental confusion
Influencing energy: encourages clarity of thought

Aquamarine
Symbology: healing benefits of spiritual truths
Influencing energy: supports faith in one's beliefs

Azurite
Symbology: high spiritual capabilities
Influencing energy: encourages confidence in personal potentiality

Aragonite
Symbology: personal growth
Influencing energy: inspires a move toward externalizing oneself; assists in developing and expanding perspectives

Aventurine
Symbology: stubbornness
Influencing energy: stimulates the attitude of acceptance

Barite
Symbology: longevity
Influencing energy: strengthens one's beliefs or perspectives; intensifies strength of personal attitudes

Beryl
Symbology: pure intentions
Influencing energy: protective qualities shielding against a sway toward ego

Black diamond
Symbology: ill-use of material wealth
Influencing energy: stimulates possessiveness

Brazilianite
Symbology: cheerfulness
Influencing energy: promotes a desire to share optimism; increases use of humor through communication

Calcite
Symbology: misunderstandings
Influencing energy: fosters situational clarity

Carnelian
Symbology: personality affectations; false expressions
Influencing energy: creates a "real" perception of self and expression of same

Cat's-eye
Symbology: a "watcher" in one's midst; personal awareness
Influencing energy: heightens observational skills

Celestine
Symbology: fragility
Influencing energy: reinforces emotional sensitivities

Cerussite
Symbology: easily manipulated
Influencing energy: increases one's recognition of manipulative individuals; energizes one's personal resolve

Chrysoberyl
Symbology: intellectual clarity
Influencing energy: bolsters clear thinking

Cinnabar
Symbology: emotional expressiveness; zest for life
Influencing energy: invigorates optimistic perspectives

Citrine
Symbology: joyful spirituality
Influencing energy: maintains an uplifting sense of faith

Coral
Symbology: living spirituality
Influencing energy: encourages the daily living of spiritual beliefs

Crown jewel
Symbology: exemplifies one's greatest desire
Influencing energy: sustains high ideals; keeps hopes energized

Cubic Zirconia

Symbology: imitation; misrepresentation; lack of genuineness

Influencing energy: induces a return to reality

Danburite

Symbology: false optimism; forced cheerfulness

Influencing energy: amplifies one's expression of true emotions

Diamond

Symbology: perfection

Influencing energy: motivates determination; influences a desire toward improvement

Diopside

Symbology: multifaceted aspect

Influencing energy: generates a recognition of opportunities or potentialities

Dioptase

Symbology: strong healing force

Influencing energy: restores self-healing effectiveness

Dravite

Symbology: depression

Influencing energy: uplifts emotional darkness and/or perceptual darkness

Emerald

Symbology: healing talent

Influencing energy: fortifies strength of personal healing capabilities

Fire agate

Symbology: confusion

Influencing energy: magnifies mental clarity

Fluorite

Symbology: protection; life irritations

Influencing energy: provides protective forces against external negativity

Garnet
Symbology: intense emotions
Influencing energy: maintains high level of convictions

Gypsum
Symbology: gentle faith; secure with beliefs
Influencing energy: reinforces security of spiritual beliefs

Hawk's-eye
Symbology: acute perception
Influencing energy: enhances perceptual abilities; heightens discernment

Heliotrope
Symbology: inherent spiritual talents
Influencing energy: amplifies effectiveness of spiritual capabilities

Hematite
Symbology: strength of one's life force
Influencing energy: bolsters perseverance

Jade
Symbology: healing qualities; protective aspects
Influencing energy: enhances personal defenses, both physical and emotional

Jasper
Symbology: life aspect capable of withdrawing negativity from self
Influencing energy: neutralizes negativity from one's life

Jet
Symbology: pessimism
Influencing energy: motivational forces which promote a balanced perspective

Kyanite
Symbology: deeper levels of an aspect; hidden elements
Influencing energy: augments analytical thought

Lapis lazuli

Symbology: deep interest in high spiritual concepts; spiritual protection

Influencing energy: magnifies spiritual confidence

Lazulite

Symbology: spiritual awareness

Influencing energy: empowers one's recognition of spiritual truths

Malachite

Symbology: healing qualities/forces in one's life

Influencing energy: vitalizes recuperative forces and assists in maintaining healthful state of being

Marcasite

Symbology: multiple spiritual elements

Influencing energy: a reminder enhancing recognition of the many spiritual opportunities we have to practice continual goodness in life

Meerschaum

Symbology: gullibility; easily manipulated

Influencing energy: assists in reinforcing self-confidence/determination

Moldavite

Symbology: uncommon knowledge; unique perspective

Influencing energy: magnifies one's ability to come to personal conclusions through thorough analyzation

Moonstone

Symbology: spiritual talents; insight

Influencing energy: strengthens energy of spiritual abilities; increases depth of insight

Morganite

Symbology: indecision

Influencing energy: revitalizes clarity of thought; quickens decision-making

Mother-of-pearl
Symbology: highest quality; best aspect of something
Influencing energy: generates increased interest in improvement

Nephrite
Symbology: healing element
Influencing energy: sustains one's self-healing capabilities

Obsidian
Symbology: protection
Influencing energy: supplements one's awareness level; fortifies empowerment

Onyx
Symbology: compassion/empathy
Influencing energy: intensifies emotional sensitivity

Opal
Symbology: truths from many sources
Influencing energy: helps in enabling one to recognize truths through various means

Pearl
Symbology: spiritual fortitude and perseverance
Influencing energy: nourishes self-confidence; revitalizes faith

Peridot
Symbology: gentle healing; long-term healing process
Influencing energy: maintains an ongoing force of healing

Petalite
Symbology: gentleness of character
Influencing energy: protects one against cynicism/emotional hardness

Phenakite
Symbology: acute discernment
Influencing energy: aids in decision-making

Rhodochrosite
Symbology: personality affectations
Influencing energy: clarifies self-perception

Rose quartz
Symbology: love
Influencing energy: heightens acceptance of others; deepens affections

Rubellite
Symbology: deep emotions (may even be hidden from self)
Influencing energy: assists emotional self-discovery/realizations

Ruby
Symbology: life force; personal energy
Influencing energy: motivational force; empowers fortitude

Sapphire
Symbology: fragile spiritual nature
Influencing energy: fortifies spiritual sensitivities

Scapolite
Symbology: gentleness of character
Influencing energy: softens personality insensitivity

Scheelite
Symbology: hidden personality
Influencing energy: encourages one to be forthright; to express true self

Seed pearl
Symbology: small imperfections
Influencing energy: facilitates a recognition of one's areas for improvement

Serpentine
Symbology: duality of character
Influencing energy: balancing forces; levels emotional polarity

Sillimanite
Symbology: indecision; cloudy thought process
Influencing energy: clarifies thinking; sharpens perception

Sinhalite
Symbology: depression
Influencing energy: uplifts personal perspectives; brightens outlook

Sodalite
Symbology: spiritual wisdom
Influencing energy: deepens spiritual conceptual comprehension

Sphalerite
Symbology: optimism
Influencing energy: upholds and energizes one's brighter attitudes

Spinel
Symbology: complexity
Influencing energy: expands one's discernment and analytical abilities

Star Sapphire
Symbology: spiritual priorities; highlighted truths
Influencing energy: heightens perception of spiritual truths

Staurolite
Symbology: perceptual density; intellectual complexity
Influencing energy: serves to fragment (untangle) complexities in life

Tanzanite
Symbology: spiritual purity; deep spiritual wisdom
Influencing energy: heightens recognition of spiritual truths and instills spiritual wisdom and insight

Tiger's-eye
Symbology: awareness; acute discernment
Influencing energy: elevates level of acuity

Titanite
Symbology: cheerfulness; light-heartedness
Influencing energy: grounding force maintaining buoyant personality

Topaz
Symbology: optimism
Influencing energy: fortifies positive outlook

Tourmaline
Symbology: healing element in one's life
Influencing energy: accentuates strength of existing healing aspects which may not be recognized as such

Turquoise
Symbology: spiritual health and well-being
Influencing energy: energizes self-healing capabilities

Vesuvianite
Symbology: unclear thought; confusion
Influencing energy: assists in clarifying thought process; helps in analyzation

Watermelon tourmaline
Symbology: healing benefits of optimism/joyfulness
Influencing energy: encourages health through the mental forces of positive thought

Wulfinite
Symbology: emotionally calming
Influencing energy: soothes erratic aura activity; stanches irritability

Zircon
Symbology: groundedness; centeredness
Influencing energy: realigns one's focus on reality

QUESTIONS ABOUT GEMSTONES

How often do the energies of gems and crystals need to be purified?

Contrary to popular belief, they don't. These are pure of themselves and *give* rather than receive. They give off their own influences. They are as a wellspring of specific and unique energy which continues to emanate from its every fiber. They do not get "dirty." They don't get "full" and they don't run out of energy from use. However, since many of you tend to have this misconception, your own thoughts can weaken the gem or stone's effectiveness through your conscious attitude about its assumed ill condition. Purify and cleanse it as much as you like, as often as you believe it needs to be done. In actuality though, you're not appreciating the true power of these elements when you feel you need to purify something that is already pure in and of itself.

I seem to have a strong affinity for jade. What does this mean for me?

Jade emanates strong energies for multiple types of healing for both physical and emotional dysfunctions. It possesses an outstanding quality which elevates it above all other healing gems and stones. This characteristic is associated with wisdom and, from ancient Egyptian times, was connected to the persona of the deity, Maat, the Goddess of Wisdom and Righteousness. She represented "balance," the balance between spiritual law and one's accumulated behavioral life experience.

Our current justice system borrowed Maat's scale to symbolize truth. So here we have a semi-precious stone which not only heals physical and emotional dysfunctions, but also lends itself to expediting an alignment of behavioral balance between experiential life activity and spirituality. Jade is a stone which emancipates us from being drawn to the darker shadows of negative attitudes, emotions, and the manner of their behavioral expression in life. Jade imparts a subtle and gentle force of impetus toward making decisions generated by wisdom instead of through knee-jerk reactions born of instantaneous emotional responses. I cannot give you a definitive answer as to what this attraction to jade means for you specifically.

Perhaps you have an inherent, strong desire for your behavioral responses to be aligned with that which is spiritually right and you feel the need for a measure of reinforcement toward this goal. Perhaps there is some hidden physical or emotional aspect in your life which you feel compelled to balance or bring into a more healthy and stable state. Only you know the real condition of self. Only you can answer this question because the clarity of its solution lies within you alone.

Is it wrong for people to take gems out of the earth?

I understand the perspective from which this question was generated. The questioner isn't quite comfortable with the idea and act of "taking" from Grandmother Earth when She's been so unconditionally giving of Her precious aspects. However, it is because of that beautiful generosity that the utilization of her aspects is so cherished. She *gives*. She *gifts* humanity with her many proffered offerings. She opens her heart, hands, and soul to us and willingly encourages the active partaking of Herself—Her very Beingness. Not only does She provide nourishing sustenance for the creatures of every shape, size, and intelligence living upon Her breast, She also bestows additional provisions for the sustained health and empowered well-being of our minds and bodies, our emotions and attitudes. And many of these aspects of Herself also carry a highly visual characteristic of precious beauty which is greatly admired and additionally utilized for adornment purposes.

No aspect of Grandmother is neutral. By this I mean to convey that no facet of Herself is without purpose or benefit. There is no element which She intended to keep hidden. She is selfless. She is eternally giving. In return we must respectfully recognize Her gifts and accept them with the reciprocal attitude of gratitude. And this last may be the crux of your initial question. Gratitude. Gratitude, not greed. Appreciation and respect, not arrogance and the attitude that we *deserve*. Gratitude and respect for Her rich gifts are shown by the manner which Her gifts are accepted. Are they received lovingly, in appreciation and respect, or are they greedily ripped from Her breast, leaving the land scarred and barren? Is Her skin repaired through replanting after Her gifts are taken or is it left flayed open like a cruel wound? The manner by which Her gifts are actualized determines whether or not humankind treats Her with love and respect.

Do simulated gemstones work as well as the real thing?

We cannot create, we can only imitate. That which Grandmother Earth creates possesses great inherent powers specific to the individual and specialized nature of each facet. Humankind can copy and imitate the visual of these, but it cannot create the energy with which the original is inherently empowered. It would be like creating a human clone—the physical body—but being unable to instill it with a soul. Because of this reality, simulated gemstones do not and cannot work as well as the genuine gifts which Grandmother creates and offers us. Oh yes, I agree that we can do a beautiful job imitating her gifts; yet they are without life, without soul. They are indeed beautiful for our eyes to behold but . . . they are also dead.

I have recurring dreams of stealing the crown jewels. What could this mean?

Let's go into this and take a look. In dream symbology, the crown jewels represent one's greatest desire. So if you "steal" them, in essence, your dream is revealing a strong desire to "force" a manifestation of your greatest desire or goal into reality. This indicates a lack of acceptance for what is. It says that you cannot wait for all intertwining facets of an event to come together naturally to create the end result you want. This dream exposes a high level of impatience which, in turn, is most likely negatively affecting other aspects of your life. Stealing what you want in life negates the value of same. What I mean by this is that the objective won't be properly formed if taken before it has been affected by the prime elements which serve in manifesting its ultimate development. Would you steal the raw and unleavened dough just to have bread? See what I'm getting at? What if your desired goal included vitally important lessons to learn while journeying along the path to acquisition? What if the means to the end turned out to be the main time frame where your "purpose" revealed itself? What if that "waiting" period between desire and attainment is meant to be the most valuable and important phase of your entire life?

You can't force goals. You can't just up and "take" whatever you want in life; it must be achieved through the means of placing one foot before the other. In this manner you accept the natural unfolding of life elements and learn from them. You grow by doing this. You mature. The idea or act of taking what you want is evidence of immaturity. It's the behavior of a small child who stomps and throws fits when he/she doesn't get his/her way . . . immediately. It's destructive behavior, destructive to self and those around you who are ultimately negatively affected by it. It's an ego thing. Me, me, me. Life desires such as future plans and goals are important to have. They give us purpose, something to look forward to and work toward, but to force these ideals is destructive and most often futile.

My suggestion to you is to give more thought to acceptance. Everything in life happens for a reason and, although that reason may not be clear to us, we still have to accept reality. We have to accept that which happens in our lives because, if it happened, we usually cannot reverse or negate events which already occurred. What we're left with is a "forward" motion.

We go forward by taking one step at a time toward our goal. Perhaps those steps have to veer off onto another trail for a time. Perhaps those steps have to slow the pace or pause in place for awhile. So what? Sometimes goals are all we have to keep us going. They give our lives meaning and purpose, something to strive and work toward. There are instances when people feel unproductive or useless after a goal has been attained. This attitude usually presents itself when a goal has not been reached through natural means and has not been realized through the process of full development.

This dream is telling you to stop being consumed by your desires and live each day as it presents itself to you. Live a full life. Appreciate each blessing which comes your way instead of ignoring it or not even recognizing it. This dream says, "relax, let your goal unfold according to its natural means." It says, "you're letting your goal make you miss out on all the beautiful facets of life!" It says, "you're making yourself (and others) miserable. Stop being so self-centered."

A friend of mine has a statue carved from hard coal and I wondered if it has negative energies?

I'm wondering if you think this because it is black? The color black doesn't always represent a dark or negative energy. Your friend most likely has a statue made of jet which is an extremely hard-packed form of coal specifically used for making jewelry and carvings. Although jet symbolizes pessimism, its healing energy emanations promote a more balanced perspective toward optimism. Likewise, black is an absorbing color and, because of this, it withdraws negativity while, at the same time, radiating positive forces. This friend's statue is a good object to have in his house and will serve as a source of emotionally balancing energies.

Can wearing a variety of gems at one time cancel out their individual effectiveness?

I found this to be a logical question based on the common understanding of gemstone energy potentiality. However, the energy strength of a stone is not diminished or negated by the close proximity of other stones of differing natures. Each stone is an entity unto itself and, therefore, emits its own, unique essence. Having other stones around it or touching it will not negatively affect its character or alter its specialized emanations. This brings to mind the question regarding the opposing effect of multiple stones: would their grouped approximation *intensify* their energies? For example, would a combination of green healing stones increase their healing influences? Not individually. Having an emerald and jade together will not create a more powerful emerald stone or jade piece. Individually they will both maintain and sustain their own energy levels, but by utilizing them together, the healing potentiality of their combined influences may intensify the healing effectiveness of an intended treatment. This is the same concept of taking two aspirins instead of one. Individually, the second aspirin does not affect the potentiality of the first, but together, their effect is intensified. But remember the important rule of thumb: more is not necessarily better.

I've noticed that American Indian jewelry frequently contains turquoise and coral. Why?

You would have to ask an American Indian jeweler that question. On a general informational level I could present a logical rationale for this combination. Turquoise symbolizes spirituality (its health and well-being within an individual) and coral symbolizes the "life" of spirituality. It makes perfect sense to combine spiritual behavior with the "living" essence of same. Sort of like the soul energizing and giving life force to spiritual attitudes and perspectives of the mind. Spirituality and the life of same—that is turquoise and coral.

Does one have to place stones on a specific body area for their healing forces to be effective?

No, but the healing influences will be more pointedly directed if they are positioned in close proximity to the physically ill or diseased area. Frequently, just the mere presence of a healing gem or stone in one's home or on his/her person in the form of jewelry can effect healing benefits without ever touching the actual diseased or ill area of the body. Healing stones placed by the bed at night, particularly on the edge of a night table near the sleeper's head, can effect a continual treatment action which is not interfered with by the individual's energy of thought patterns. Another highly effective healing methodology which few people use or have even given a thought to utilizing, is combining water with healing stones. In this method, the gem is placed in clear bathwater (without any additives such as oils) and the individual reaps the benefits of the water conducting the gem's energy emanations over the entire body. This manifests a "flowing" energy about the individual and creates an entire immersion of self into the waters charged with the gem's influence. Regardless of what method is utilized, the gem will emanate its influence no matter where it is placed in the home.

Why is amber considered a natural gem?

It's considered a natural gem because it's one of Grandmother's natural beauties. It's a fossil resin which frequently contains bits of organic matter (insects) within its formed substance. Friction applied to amber can also create a negative charge. It acts as an insulator which is why it symbolizes loyalty and influences a sense of assuredness. By insulating an individual against the outside negative influences from others, it protects against attitudes counter to one's own which could serve to bring about personal doubts or a questioning of self. Grandmother's gifts are natural. They come from within Her beingness and are comprised of Her very essence; therefore, all of Her physical manifestations from this beautiful beingness can be considered to be gems. Yet humankind has chosen to separately distinguish what it calls "gems" by classifying Her gifts into differentiating categories. Amber is a natural gem gift as much as an emerald or ruby is.

Would it be wrong to have an engagement ring of cubic zirconium?

I don't see any reason for it to be wrong. An engagement ring is only a symbol. It is not used as a healing gem or for any influential energy purposes. Cubic zirconium stones are beautiful and quite a bit less expensive than diamonds. I see no reason to have any guilt over choosing these over the real thing. Since this inquiry came from a man, I do suggest the decision to go with the cubic zirconium is a mutually shared one by both parties. I've noticed that society appears to have its priorities skewed. The generally held attitude toward cubic zirconium used in a wedding set is that of disfavor, more accurately, it is unthinkable. Why? If the wedding set represents the "love" each partner has for the other, do you think a mere stone is going to increase or decrease that level of affection? Are you of the opinion that an "imitation" or synthetic stone will lessen or demean the "quality" of that love? If that's what you think then you are greatly mistaken. Just as a bigger stone doesn't represent a larger amount of love, neither does an imitation stone symbolize a false love. People need to understand that an engagement ring or a wedding ring set is only a *symbol*. It's only a "tradition" of society which makes it a physical accoutrement of marriage. Is a love less real—have less depth—without a ring? Of course not. Is a marriage not a marriage without rings? How silly an idea that is. Symbology. It's only symbology. And a *physical* object cannot begin to adequately represent that which dwells within the heart. To bring my point home . . . an engagement ring made of a cigar band or an aluminum can's pull ring can be just as meaningful as a two-carat diamond. Society has a fascination with "stuff." The bigger the better; the more expensive, the greater the affection; but that's false thinking. We need to get back to the importance and priority of the inner world of emotions where expressed actions and behavior become the true symbols of love.

I want to heal myself but can't seem to get past a spell of negative thought. Any suggestions regarding this problem?

The answer is contained within your own question. Your negativity has, in essence, placed a "spell" on blocking the effectiveness of the gems you're using. While the gems are emanating strong influential energies toward healing, your negative thoughts are blasting back out of your aura and negating the incoming forces. Remember that the mental is a powerful force. Thoughts are things. Your negative thoughts are not actually creating a spell *per se*, but they are blocking incoming energies and neutralizing their influence. This is not to infer that negative energy negates positive energy. I'm not saying that. But you are sending out strong negative vibrations which prevent the positive, healing influences of the stones from an optimum level of effectiveness upon your being. When one wishes to participate in the process of performing a healing, he/she needs to be emotionally balanced and mentally clear. Both the practitioner and patient need to be in an open and receptive frame of mind. To attempt a healing when negative attitudes abound in strength, the healing process can be a complete waste of time. If you can't manage to control the negative thoughts and still wish to attempt a healing, I suggest you add a watermelon tourmaline to your grouping of gems. This little seemingly innocuous stone has the wonderful ability to both heal *and* counter negative thought.

Is it okay for marcasite stones to be set in gold?

Sure it's okay, but they're more effective set in silver or platinum. You see, marcasite symbolizes spiritual elements and silver does, too. Gold represents the materialism of the physical. They don't mix well because individually they represent two separate and completely different planes of existence and their counter ideologies.

What is your favorite gemstone?

Normally I wouldn't answer this, but it's been asked a lot. My strongest attractions are to red garnet and clear emerald. I have a strong affinity with jade.

What is a "record" crystal?

You won't find such a mineral as a "record" crystal in a technical mineralogy text because the concept is a New Age one. Some people believe that certain crystals contain the coded records of creation within the geometric matrix of specific crystals. A mineralogist will snicker at this belief while the new agers will be held in awe over it. As with any subject matter, you'll find a wide scope of associated belief systems ranging from hard reality to the outrageous. The idea of a crystal containing creation records is not one I personally give credence to.

Can gems be programmed?

Programmed for what? Gems, in and of themselves, possess their own energy influences which make each one unique. Each one is a technical marvel of creation. To assume that humans have power to alter or affect those energies is a bit arrogant.

What is a teaching stone?

You're asking for the name of a specific type of stone, but there is no such thing as a particular species of teaching stone. They all teach us something. All of nature is a teacher. All of nature provides us with important concepts which, in turn, teach valuable lessons. Again, the idea of a specific "teaching" stone is a new age concept but not one of true reality.

Does the color of a diamond affect its power?

No. The strength of a gem's influence is generated from the source of its energy. That energy comes from its composition, not its grade of quality. Color does not interfere with its core of inherent energy by lessening or diminishing it. A diamond is a diamond and contains the influencing energy of a diamond no matter what its quality. This is a general misconception people seem to have regarding gems. There is a belief that the gem must be perfect in order to be effective. This isn't so. It isn't so because the influence emanates from its composition, and is not affected by its condition. To think that a gem is not effective just because it's not in perfect condition isn't an example of rational thought. Does a car not work just because it has a few dings on its fender or is marred by dirt or bird droppings? A raw gem has as much energy influence as a processed one. An emerald doesn't have to have a jeweler's emerald cut to effectively heal. Likewise, a diamond which still has raw coal material attached has the same powerful force of energy as one cleaned, cut, and polished. So you see, the simple aspect of a stone's "color" is not a factor associated with a gem's effectiveness.

Is a crystal's power increased when placed in a wand?

Absolutely not. A crystal is a crystal all by itself. I'm personally confounded and dismayed to see so many folks who have a penchant for dressing up stones, as if these additions serve to increase their power. If anything, the "dressing" can manifest a mind-set whereby the individual's thoughts associated with the accouterments actually deflect the pure energy influence of the stone itself. What I'm saying is that cluttered perceptual aspects can alter one's original intent. When an object is "dressed up," that object looses its central focus, because the focus is shifted to the reason for its accouterments; for example, ceremonial magic. In this manner, the focus is altered in a manner which centers on an individual or on the compound aspects of a ritual rather than where it belongs—on the crystal itself. Conceptually, the reality of crystal and other gemstones' utilization has been severely misunderstood. The reality of their beautiful, inherent essences has been cluttered by people's desire for ceremony and ritual. Gems and crystals need no human hocus-pocus to make them work better or increase their power. These natural gifts of our Grandmother need nothing humans could add to them for alleged purposes of enhancement. Humans have not the ability to enhance the inherent power contained within nature's facets. So why the wands, the rituals, the dressings when all aspects of nature's raw beingness are so incredibly pure and powerful all by themselves? What is it about nature that you don't understand that you have such a strong desire to dress it up?

Does the size of a gem make a difference in its effectiveness?

What is this continual fascination and worry over "size" of everything in life? No, size makes no difference in a stone's effectiveness. Bigger is definitely not always better.

Which stones are best to actualize past-life recall?

That's quite a question. It supports the fact that people are looking outside themselves for that which lies within. The complete record of all an individual's past lives is contained within the consciousness. The consciousness is one's spirit totality. The consciousness is like a constantly growing crystal whereby each incarnated life creates another facet of the main crystal body. Our consciousness is that spirit crystal. All we have to do is go within to recapture those individual experiential memories which each crystal facet holds. What is this idea of a special stone actualizing this process? What is it in human nature that creates such a strong desire to look all about for powers which are already within self? Is it that people are lazy? That they want something touchable and handed to them, so they don't have to expend personal energy to achieve goals? Is it that people haven't yet learned or understood that the human mind is more powerful than any gem or stone?

Memories of all past-life experiences are contained within one's consciousness. Certain influences from these lives cross over (or bleed) into the current experience by way of specific attractions, skills, interests, and relationships. My concern is that so many people feel such a strong desire to know who they were in the past when that information is not vital to present-day function. In fact, it can hamper the natural unfolding of one's current life. What's important is to live in the now. Each moment is a precious gift from God and when those moments are not utilized to recognize and appreciate the many beautiful blessings and opportunities which present themselves, then life is not lived with open eyes and in awareness. The past is recorded past—history. Be who you are today. Develop that unique individual in a spiritual manner. Today's life will one day be a past life. What you do today, the accomplishments and behavior, will determine the shape and form, the clarity and characteristics of the crystal facet now materializing from within your spirit's consciousness totality. What stone is best to actualize past-life recall? The greatest, most powerful crystal of all . . . you.

Is it harmful to be a hard rock miner?

Other than it being hard work, no. This question was generated from the idea of it possibly being harmful to be continually exposed to the multiple influences from a great diversity of minerals. No, although hard rock miners may appear to be bombarded by multiple mineral influences in a simultaneous manner, these emanations are not harmful in any way because nature is beneficial in character. I thought this question showed deep thought because it didn't come from a hard rock miner as you'd expect. Being exposed to a variety of raw minerals on a daily basis has no ill effects from the minerals themselves. What could cause harm would be unhealthful working conditions in the mine operations or an individual's psychological attitude regarding being underground. Specific to the spirit of this question, a jeweler could be equated to the hard rock miner who is constantly exposed to a wide variety of gems. On a daily basis, jewelers handle and work with all types of gemstones without being negatively affected by the exposure. In addition, they also handle various types of metals such as silver, gold, and platinum. This type of work is incredibly hard on the hands and, over time, can develop into physical problems with fingers and wrists, but there are no negative effects directly caused by the stones themselves.

ROCKS

Agate
Symbology: multiple talents
Influencing energy: assists in recognition of personal skills

Aggregate
Symbology: need to consider the whole rather than focusing on the parts
Influencing energy: brings clarity to analytical thought

Anhydrite
Symbology: unessential aspects
Influencing energy: intensifies mental focus on the basic elements of an issue

Anthracite
Symbology: impetus; encouragement
Influencing energy: supports drive; heightens goal orientation

Basalt
Symbology: path direction
Influencing energy: highlights main focus; assists in perceiving unessential aspects to one's path which may otherwise divert and detain advancement

Breccia
Symbology: beauty through gentleness
Influencing energy: teaches the power of gentleness

Feldspar
Symbology: transmitting qualities; communication
Influencing energy: facilitates more effective transmission of ideas

Fieldstone
Symbology: that which provides "building" or "developmental" aspects as opportunities are taken advantage of
Influencing energy: enhances recognition of valuable opportunities

Firebrick
Symbology: emotional protection/insulation
Influencing energy: helps prevent personal internalization of another's behavior or emotionality

Flagstone
Symbology: specific life aspects which serve to "pave" one's way
Influencing energy: magnifies one's direction or life course

Flint
Symbology: quick response/reaction time
Influencing energy: encourages awareness of explosive situations

Fossil
Symbology: preserved immutable aspects/truths
Influencing energy: heightens recognition of reality; elevates perceptual acuity

Geode
Symbology: hidden truths/beauty
Influencing energy: intensifies awareness; helps to understand true power and beauty

Gneiss
Symbology: extraneous aspects; affectations
Influencing energy: increases ability to see through surface aspects and into the core element; guards against falling victim to manipulation

Granite
Symbology: solid foundation
Influencing energy: aids in ability to distinguish between reality and fantasy, solid truths from fiction; fortifies accurate insight

Lava
Symbology: inner strength; self-confidence
Influencing energy: instills faith in self which insulates against self-doubt or loss of confidence and perseverance

Limestone

Symbology: spiritual foundation; proof of beliefs

Influencing energy: acts as a verifying element in one's life; rekindles and stabilizes one's personal perspectives

Lodestone

Symbology: strong attraction; compelling force/drive

Influencing energy: serves as a powerful impetus; strengthens determination

Marble

Symbology: lasting effort or aspect; enduring

Influencing energy: reinforces determination/perseverance; affects a sense of rightness in spite of associated complexities of involved elements

Mica

Symbology: "shiny" bits and pieces of joyful moments we experience while making our life journey; blessings

Influencing energy: augments ability to recognize life's opportunities and blessings which would otherwise pass unnoted

Obsidian

Symbology: higher spiritual concepts; deeper spiritual philosophy

Influencing energy: clarifies spiritual concepts which are perceived as having complexity; contributes to understanding the beauty of spiritual simplicity; increases incidences of spiritual insight—The Knowing

Pegmatite

Symbology: hidden value

Influencing energy: encourages recognition and appreciation of real value and power; instills a greater measure of personal wisdom

Pipestone

Symbology: spiritual sacredness

Influencing energy: amplifies understanding of spiritual sacredness and deepens respect for same; intensifies spiritual tolerance for different spiritual beliefs held by others

Pumice

Symbology: a rough life aspect; difficulties

Influencing energy: imparts a soothing force; calming; solace; tends to ease one over the rough waters of life

Pyroxenite

Symbology: complexity; multi-elements associated with a single aspect

Influencing energy: helps to widen one's perspective; exposes all aspects of a situation, relationship, or condition

Quartz

Symbology: purity of spiritual truths

Influencing energy: advocates a heightened perception and recognition of true spiritual realities

Rhyolite

Symbology: insulating qualities; permanence; enduring

Influencing energy: enriches sense of individuality; subsidizes sense of assuredness

River rock

Symbology: spiritual simplicity; uncomplicated concepts

Influencing energy: simplifies perception of complex spiritual ideologies

Rose quartz

Symbology: joy and humility associated with one's spiritual gifts

Influencing energy: instills a proper perspective with respect to one's spiritual talents; heightens personal joy after sharing spiritual talents; increases personal appreciation for ability and opportunities to practice unconditional goodness

Sandstone

Symbology: weak foundation; lacking strong basics

Influencing energy: helps to expose illogical or irrational thought; brings clarity to analytical thinking; reveals erroneous qualities to a basic premise

Slate

Symbology: protection; communication

Influencing energy: fortifies one's personal defenses; enhances ability to properly relate ideas of concepts to others

Soapstone

Symbology: understanding; acceptance

Influencing energy: heightens rationality; intensifies one's ability to cope with difficult situations

QUESTIONS ABOUT ROCKS

Is a geode's influence stronger when left in its natural state or opened?

Opened. When a geode is opened, its energy influences are released so their full potentiality can be emanated outward. A natural geode is like a present still hidden within a wrapped gift box. The wrapping needs to come off and the box opened in order for the contents to be recognized, utilized, and appreciated.

Can rocks be magical like at Stonehenge?

Magical? Let's not equate the sciences of physics and astronomy with magic; we've grown too intelligent for that. Precise placements of monoliths by the ancients for the purpose of astronomical alignments were not perceived as being magical by the original architects, so why would we now make presumptions that any form of magic was involved in the practice? It appears to be common for people to make assumptions which involve the esoteric when no other rationale is deduced. A lack of understanding and clear comprehension doesn't make something mystical or esoteric, though humankind loves to assume that it does. If people can't figure out a reasonable or technical explanation for an event or situation they resort to the terms "miracle," or "mystical," or whatever. The element of fire was probably viewed by the cavemen as some kind of magic or miracle. I would hope that the people experiencing yet another millennium have developed beyond this primitive consciousness. There was no magic associated with the monoliths of Stonehenge and other like locales. Since the beginning of time, ancient peoples have arranged rocks in a multitude of designs for an equally varied number of reasons depending on cultural belief systems. Look at the American Indian's medicine wheel for another example. The Stonehenge monoliths are exactly how they are for astronomical reasons. They have no inherent magic or "special powers" associated with them.

I was under the impression that it was detrimental to live on old magma or lava. Am I way off base with this theory?

We need to get more specific here. There is hardened lava and then there is lava as in "lava fields." In one of my Colorado locations I had a cabin which was built on an old lava field which extended for miles and miles in all directions. The soil there was unlike the general Rocky Mountain soil of Colorado, which is comprised of a high percentage of crumbled granite, mica, quartz crystal, and glistening pyrite. This lava field soil was rich and black. It was like a fertile humus full of nutrients. This is wonderful to live on. I'm not saying this because I once lived on it, I'm saying it because it's true. That sort of soil is ideal for gardens—botanicals grow like crazy in it. So no, living on old lava fields is not detrimental. Now if you're talking about real hardened lava, well, I can't imagine anyone wanting to have a dwelling on that. Don't forget, though, the Pacific Rim islands were made of growing lava formations. Hawaii and its neighboring islands are still growing, but they are also still experiencing recent lava flows which are hazardous.

Is petrified wood really a stone or rock?

Though it definitely has the feel of stone, it's still comprised of its original organic material. This inherent organic material is not lost over the time of its preservation process.

What are Standing Stones? Are they made of a specific type of rock?

Standing Stones are the voices of nature's living consciousness. These are unique nature "receivers" which hold and have the capability of transmitting vibrational energies of thought to those who are spiritually sensitive to their fine rate of movement and sound. They are not specific to an ethnic group and can be comprised of a wide variety of rock.

Do pebbles found on beaches give off any specialized influences?

Oh yes, they are as spiritual lodestones and wonderfully effective emotional tranquilizers. They relieve stress when utilized as a companion piece to hold in one's hand and smooth with the fingers. Forget the worry-beads and find yourself a good, smooth beach pebble instead.

I have a quartz crystal that has been artificially colored. Does that negatively affect its energy?

Artificial color enhancement does not negatively affect the crystal's inherent quality or natural characteristics of energy influence; neither does it positively affect its nature. Artificial is just what it says—artificial—and therefore has no natural characteristic components of its own to impart to the base mineral or element. Your crystal remains unchanged regardless of added color.

Does the predominance of a specific geologic rock in a geographic region affect the locale's overall energy?

Yes, all facets of nature affect each other, including the human aspects. As an example of this, people living where there is a great amount of naturally occurring marble will generally tend to have a stronger sense of perseverance than the norm. They'll experience a strengthening in their determination and goal-focused ideals. Those living in a geographical region rich in mica will usually be more light-hearted and accepting of life. It's important to remember that all of life is interconnected; subtly, yet tightly, intertwined. The great, living Web of Life pulses with the influencing energies of every life cell of each living species. Our energies affect the nature surrounding us just as that emanating essense of nature affects us. We are all cells of the Living, Divine Consciousness. We are . . . each other.

When a sculptor creates a piece of artwork from stone, does the stone's energy influence the artist in any way? The viewer?

This is an interesting question. The answer is yes. Over time, the experienced sculptor becomes intimate with the innate qualities of the various stones. For instance, alabaster will have a different characteristic than marble. The artist carefully chooses his/her medium for the specific qualities the stone will lend to the creation. These qualities are not always chosen for ease of creative workability, but for the influence the stone's nature will emanate from the completed sculpture. This then gives an important aspect of added dimensional depth to the finished piece, one which has the potentiality of striking the sensitive core of the viewer and evoking an emotional response.

I love stone cottages. Are there any negative aspects to living in one?

Though I've heard it said that stone is cold, both physically and emotionally, there is no negative influential effect from its energy. I lived in a tiny stone cabin, and it was the coziest little place to be. It wasn't constructed of the "river rock" most folks visualize when hearing the term, "stone cabin," it was made of Colorado granite stones. It sparkled with bits of mica, quartz, and pyrite when the moonlight touched it. The bright sunlight made it warm and the stones took in the heat and held it like a burning ember. It was a good place. Stone is enduring. It is of the earth. And when utilizing local rocks, the structure takes on a more natural, vibrationally aligned essence which is likened to pulling up the ends of Grandmother Earth's robe and wrapping yourself in it. It's wonderfully comforting.

Do rocks contain cellular memory?

Cellular memory. Every singular cell of every kind holds memory of itself and its purpose. If this wasn't so, liver cells would attempt to be gallbladder cells or heart muscle cells. It is the concept of cell memory which maintains the ordered spectrum of our universe. All matter is energy. This energy has motion. You may not be able to visually perceive the molecular movements, but that doesn't mean there's no cellular activity going on or that an object is inert. We also know that *thoughts* are things, too. Thoughts have energy, therefore, thoughts can affect matter—the living cells of matter. All of life is interconnected through cellular memory and the emanating influences with which all matter permeates the fine strands of the great Web of Life.

What influence would a meteorite rock have?

One of the universe. A meteorite contains a different cell memory than the geologic elements of earth because it has absorbed multifaceted aspects of its journey through the universe. This then means that its influence would be of a more spiritual nature, in that it has "experienced" and been exposed to the wisdom whispered through the great, vibrational hum of life—the music of the spheres. Though crystals seem to be popularly touted as the most powerful "magical" rocks to possess, that is a widespread error in perception—a misconception—for they are merely of this singular earthly planet. Meteorites far surpass the influences of crystals because they are of the universe and, being such, contain universal facets which no earthly element is capable of. We must remember that the popularity of a concept doesn't necessarily make it correct. Believing in and holding to generally held theorems can prevent intellectual and experiential expansion from occurring. Maintaining that crystals are the ultimate power rock inhibits one's opportunistic receptivity for gaining expanded knowledge. In reality, the influences from crystals can't hold a candle to a meteorite's powerful, spiritual emanations. What are these?

A meteorite's energy stimulates spiritual curiosity and prompts one to look past man-made dogma and discover that which has been imprinted on the memory cells of the universe since the time of creation. Meteorites open one to awe-filled epiphanies, sudden flashes of spiritual inspiration, and strengthen the connective thread of one's consciousness to that of the Divine Mind.

Can the energy of a rock be harmed by destructive mining methods?

No, because the rock's inherent composition is not altered. The rock itself is not harmed, but destructive mining methods do harm the environment surrounding the rock's locale. Just as clear-cut lumber harvesting negatively impacts the environment, destructive mining also leaves its open wound upon Grandmother's soft breast and injects poison into her veins.

How do rocks feel about being mined?

Exposed! Seriously, I'm not sure we can equate precise human emotions to rocks, but it seems to me that they'd enjoy every opportunity to share their beneficial influences. All of nature is interactive in one way or another, every cell has the potentiality to affect every other living cell. Besides feeling suddenly naked, I suppose mined rocks like having the opportunity to be useful and appreciated.

Speaking of rocks, is there an underground civilization currently existing?

Not like humankind *above* ground. Many natures have intelligence and souls. Many different natures exist concurrently with humankind. Many of these have been relegated to myth and tales of fairies. The myth evaporates as soon as you've heard a fairy tell a tale.

I have a large piece of raw pipestone which I plan to carve. Is it wrong for me to have this?

No, why would you think this? You also said it was given to you as a gift. I'm sure you'll turn it into something beautiful. Let's not get too carried away with ideological strictures regarding who should have what. Grandmother's gifts are for everyone. She doesn't pick and choose who she gifts them to or designates them for. She is all-inclusive. We are all her children.

I live in an area loaded with basalt. Does this rock represent a possible future danger for the region?

If you're wondering if there will be the possibility for future activity, I suppose that potentiality exists for all former lava flow areas. Old volcanos can become active again, yet all the hot springs in your area indicate a geothermically energetic region. Just by that fact alone, I'd say the possibility certainly exists for future activity to resume.

Do different fossils emit different energies?

Only minutely. Fossils are a conglomerate category of rock symbolizing truths which remain unchanged throughout time. Generally they represent a composite message of immutability and stability.

Pumice is such an ugly rock that it's hard to believe that it could have beneficial qualities.

That's because human nature tends to equate beauty with admirable qualities. All aspects of nature possess positive facets. Sometimes the less attractive they are, the more power their influence holds. People say that beauty is in the eye of the beholder, but those who aren't drawn to beauty reap the most benefits from all life has to offer.

Slate seems so cold and lacks characteristic distinction. How can it emanate any influential energies?

Again, I have to remind you that appearances are deceiving. And why isn't the appearance of slate a distinctive characteristic unique unto itself? Humanity is so full of preconceived notions about beauty and character that it saddles itself with a self-imposed myopic perspective on life. This narrow perspective prevents a true appreciation of nature's unlimited facets. Slate possesses a highly effective influence of protective qualities. Slate should not be overlooked just because it is not perceived as being "distinctive" in character.

Soapstone is more easily carved than other rock materials. Is there some particular figure which releases its energy more than another?

No, because a rock's energy emanates from its inherent composition, not from its shape or condition. You can carve a statuette of Jesus or Yoda and both will emit the stone's exact influence in equal strength. Shape has no bearing and in no way affects a rock's energy.

Is river rock the best type of rock to build a stone house of?

Generally, it's more convenient and cheaper to build of a type of rock which is indigenous to your locale; but personally, I believe that it's more advantageous to choose otherwise if one is drawn to a particular kind of rock. I favor river rock because of its aesthetic qualities of rounded smoothness which gives the sense of gentleness and serenity rather than the sharp harshness other types of rock can physically convey. Also, the river rock represents spiritual simplicity which is directly related to my goal in conveying spiritual concepts. The river rock just seems to more accurately align with my personality more than other types of stone. I would suggest that one should utilize whatever type of rock one is most attracted to, not an attraction of appearance, but an attraction of personal draw despite its physical appearance. While some folks will be drawn to a specific kind of brick, others will choose moss rock or granite. It's really up to the individual; there is not any definitively, prescribed type.

A friend gave me a bracelet made of various agate stones. In what way will this piece of jewelry help me? Aren't these stones just pretty rocks?

Well, they are very pretty rocks, but they also have inherent influential energies emanating from their composition. They help one to recognize his/her hidden skills. They assist in the development of these by way of strengthening one's self-confidence in personal abilities and special talents. They contribute to an expansion of ways in which these skills can be effectively utilized.

I was told that a piece of flint was good to carry in one's pocket. Why?

Whoever told you this might have felt you needed assistance in quickening your reaction time to situations, because this is flint's specific influence. It sharpens perception and cognizance of potentially explosive situations while they're in the active process of building. So many times we get caught up in circumstances brought on by others and we don't recognize where it's all heading until it's too late and we find ourselves right in the middle of someone else's conflict. Flint helps to shed insight on these types of developments. In other words, it aids in keeping us from being involuntarily drawn into other people's business and problems.

Are stones with natural holes through them special "healing" stones?

No, they're merely stones with naturally occurring holes through them. We must be careful not to attribute esoteric meaning to elements in nature and life. Society has a fascination with the mystic and mysterious. It tends to think the beauty of nature has to be glamorized according to human criteria rather than being recognized for its simplistic beauty of self.

METALS

Aluminum

Symbology: reflection

Influencing energy: deepens contemplative reach

Antimony

Symbology: a multifaceted aspect

Influencing energy: heightens knowledge of multiple ways to utilize skills

Bismuth

Symbology: a multifaceted aspect (same as antimony)

Influencing energy: heightens knowledge of multiple ways to utilize skills

Bronze

Symbology: beauty of blending specific life aspects; preservation

Influencing energy: encourages a recognition of true value in life; heightens effectiveness of skills when combined in an interrelated manner of utilization

Cadmium

Symbology: an added aspect; an external facade

Influencing energy: encourages the utilization of positive thinking to enhance relationships or situations

Chromium

Symbology: endurance

Influencing energy: promotes determination and perseverance

Copper

Symbology: communication

Influencing energy: increases communication effectiveness

Gold

Symbology: financial and material aspects in one's life

Influencing energy: instills foundational confidence

Gold dust

Symbology: material benefits attained from one's applied efforts

Influencing energy: enhances appreciation of perseverance and hard work

Iron

Symbology: strength

Influencing energy: empowers inner fortitude

Lead

Symbology: potential negative aspect

Influencing energy: heightens recognition of potentially negative or dangerous elements to a situation or relationship

Magnesium

Symbology: enlightenment; clear sight

Influencing energy: clarifies rationale and reason; inspiration

Mercury

Symbology: vacillation; fluctuation

Influencing energy: amplifies one's ability to perceive impending shifts in attitude or situational developments

Nickel

Symbology: alternatives; a replacement method

Influencing energy: assists one in recognizing and exploring alternate courses of action or potential solutions

Palladium

Symbology: impetus; an aspect which motivates

Influencing energy: stimulates forward progress; inspires confidence

Platinum

Symbology: multiple opportunities

Influencing energy: facilitates inspiration; subsidizes one's utilization of skills through multiple means

Pyrite

Symbology: impulsiveness

Influencing energy: increases cautiousness in regard to jumping to conclusions or tending to not think things out

Silver

Symbology: spiritual elements in life

Influencing energy: deepens one's experiential appreciation of life's spiritual aspects

Tin

Symbology: an inferior life aspect; insubstantiality; a weak facet

Influencing energy: reinforces one's inner strength and conviction; sharpens recognition of ineffective methods or weak rationale

Titanium

Symbology: inner strength; endurance; perseverance

Influencing energy: empowers resolve; deepens self-assurance

Zinc

Symbology: protection; a protective measure

Influencing energy: augments one's personal protective elements; increases protective inner strengths

QUESTIONS ABOUT METALS

Which is more beneficial to wear, silver or gold?

The point of this question isn't which metal carries the greatest general benefit, but which is right for you personally. Gold instills foundational confidence and is associated with the physical world and matter. Silver brings about a deeper appreciation of spiritual aspects and is associated with the spiritual world and its concepts. Both emanate beneficial influences and, depending on your perspective or emotional mood when getting dressed, you will most likely naturally reach for whatever piece of jewelry that most closely aligns with your aura's current state.

Should we be saving gold for the future?

It's a good idea to have some gold put away with a stash of cash against periods of future disarray within the financial arena. This stash should already be a building nest-egg as part of survival preparations. If the Y2K Bug isn't fixed by the year 2000, every operational process which runs with a computer chip will be useless. That means banks, ATMs, computer-generated salary and Social Security checks, direct deposits, etc. Gas pumps may not work and computer-operated electric power plants may shut down for a time. But it's important to understand that this glitch could happen at any time. It's not just a millennium situation. There are various causal factors which could shut down society's computers. If you have a bit of foresight and have that "stash-of-cash" I keep suggesting, you'll be far better off by being prepared for such an event. Now, when I say that gold is a good idea, I don't necessarily mean big, heavy bars of it. You can buy it in coins and small nuggets. This concept is a checkmate against the future possibility of the dollar losing all value. If you're of a mind to plan for such future possibilities, then plan for all contingencies.

I live in a gold-rich region. Is gold dust worth panning for?

Most gold-rich regions have been fairly well worked by now, but you can find streams which wash down placer gold which collects in bends and beneath rocks. No matter what the form, all gold has value. The flakes take a great deal of time to collect and separate out, but hey, you just might find that nugget. Besides, it's great fun and it gets you out in nature for awhile. Don't let anyone laugh over your efforts; at least you're being creative and adventurous. Just don't confuse the gold flakes with the pyrite (fool's gold) which the streams are loaded with. Pyrite will *sparkle* like a Fourth of July sparkler, but real gold will have a dull *shine*.

Are mercury dental fillings harmful?

Yes, they sure are. There are many popular technical books written on this subject. It doesn't take much research to get the information on this. I see no point in going into all the technicalities here when there is so much already published. As a guideline, remember that potent metals do not belong in the body because they emit harmful elements which adversely affect the systems, especially the highly sensitive brain which absorbs the trace elements of metals into its cellular matter. Now I want to clarify another spin-off aspect of this issue. For those of you with plates or pins in your bodies due to orthopedic surgery, this mercury question does not apply to you because those appliances are composed of different material. This question was specifically associated with dental fillings containing mercury.

Is it a good idea to consider geologic metal content of the geographical area one is contemplating a relocation to?

Absolutely. Not only the natural geologic content of elements, but also do a little research regarding mining operations that may or may not still be in operation. Some geographic areas are on the government's Superfund clean-up list because of past chemical dumping into water sources and soil. For example, when I lived in Leadville, Colorado, I heard a television news report about a survey showing that the children living there had a higher content of lead in their systems due to the silver content of the soil and the ensuing mining that disturbed the ground. One of my daughters had come down with a serious problem in all her joints. After moving away, it cleared up within four months. The spirit of this question is "awareness." Have awareness when searching for a region to relocate to. Make astute observations. Ask questions and do a bit of research. There is far more beneath a new locale than the surface, exterior beauty of high mountains, stark desert, or beaches showered with sea spray. Do your homework and you won't be disappointed.

I bought some American Indian jewelry with the turquoise set in nickel instead of silver. Does that affect the influence of the stones in any way?

No, because the stones emanate their influences from their own inherent composition, not from whatever setting they may be in. Nickel won't usually tarnish like silver does. Though you may have thought you were purchasing silver, the nickel is easier to care for. And since nickel metal heightens one's recognition of alternatives in life, perhaps it was destiny rather than the mistake you're perceiving it to be.

I heard that carbon steel helps sinuses. Comment?

Unalloyed carbon steel gets its influencing properties from its high content of carbon which, in its natural state of coal, produces charcoal, graphite, and diamonds. It is this content of the steel which the influence emanates from. The suggestion of using carbon "steel" comes from its durability and lasting character. One couldn't very easily carry around a piece of raw coal all the time for this purpose. Just as with all matter, there is a duality to its properties. The carbon component in an element can cause harmful effects if utilized in excessive amounts.

It seems to me that metals are generally harmful for the body. True?

The key word in this statement is "generally." And I would agree with the correspondent on this. Metals have a wide variety of beneficial inherent influences, yet because of their hardness, also have reflective and deflective characteristics. These attributes distinguish metals from all other material composition in that they have the potentiality to interfere with a calm and serene atmosphere by reflecting vibrational energies in erratic patterns. This activity is not readily noticeable with jewelry as much as it is with types of metal furnishings such as steel file cabinets, bookcases, chrome tables, brass lamps, and decorative items such as bronze statues. These cause a "spiking" action which energy vibrations spear off of. For example, the reaction between metal objects and human vibrational energies could be better understood if we envisioned the emotional mood differentiation between sitting in a log cabin in front of a crackling fireplace on a cold, snowy evening and that of sitting in a room surrounded by nothing but wall-to-wall mirrors. The wood of the log walls *absorbs* vibrations and creates a soft, quiet atmosphere as contrasted to the spearing reflections of *deflecting* vibrations, which cause irritability, anxiety, and nervousness. If one could physically see the spiking vibrations which metal continually throws about, you would observe a room full of what might look like a network or web of laser rays that you'd have to pass through. And, in doing so, your own body is then bombarded by these erratic energies. Metal is alright to wear as jewelry, but not recommended for furniture.

When wearing gold, does the carat affect the metal's level of influence?

Sure it does. Gold normally comes in 10, 14, 18, and 24 carats. The last being the pure grade of bouillon. The 24-carat grade is very soft and it's the reason gold is hardened for durability by creating the other grades which have copper and silver added. The lower the carat number the less amount of pure gold is contained within the object. The influencing energy emanating from 24-carat gold will be much stronger than that from a 10 carat.

Aluminum has many valuable uses, yet it's not good to cook with. Why?

The same reason why mercury has valuable uses yet it doesn't belong in people's teeth. There is no element which is all bad. I want to clarify that misconception. Some metals have adverse affects when utilized in an improper manner. Aluminum is not healthy when brought into contact with any mouth tissue or skin cells to absorb, yet the metal is wonderful for a wide variety of other uses. Another example is asbestos. It's a great insulator, but not good to breathe into our lung tissue or get in our skin. The key is proper utilization of Grandmother's natural gifts.

Are copper bracelets healthful to wear?

Because of copper's inherent quality of conductivity, folks have assumed that wearing it will increase circulation, thereby alleviating blocked energy channels leading to arthritis. This seems reasonable in theory, but technically it isn't effective for the abovementioned purpose.

Does zinc really help defend against getting a cold?

Zinc is a metallic mineral found in trace amounts within the body. It can aid in the treatment of colds as much as Vitamin C can. The important fact to remember is that "more is not always better." Fads come and go. In the meantime, people rush out to buy and ingest mega amounts of the Cure That Wasn't and end up with a dangerously high level of mineral that was only meant to be a trace amount for balance.

Beauty from Her Opened Hands

Grandmother has always embraced us through the gifts of Herself. She reaches Her arms out and gently unfurls Her aged fingers to lovingly present us with offerings of the joyful bounties of flowers and trees. These, so plentiful, fall from her palms and cover the receiving ground as living adornments upon the hem of Her flowing gown. And so She has anointed us with Her blessings of everlasting fruitfulness and beauty which daily presents us with a multitude of opportunities to experience heartfelt joy and wonder. Yet how infrequently precious time is taken from humanity's hectic life to slow the harried pace enough to notice these many blessings and truly admire them with deep appreciation and thankfulness. Oh yes, an old oak is noticed on a steaming, hot day when it offers cool and shady respite for the family picnic, and the anniversary bouquet of roses is joyfully accepted as a proclamation of another's love, but what of all the other gifts which we're continually surrounded by, but are rarely taken note of in passing? The gracefulness of the weeping willow sweeping her hair over the mirrored surface of a reflecting pond, golden wheat rippling in hushed whispers to the wind, fruit trees heavy with nutritional bounty, wildflowers blanketing a mountain meadow in a riot of colorful splendor, a brilliant red blossom on a desert cactus, all there for human enjoyment, gifts freely offered to the perceptive and appreciative individual. Though we're aware of the eye-catching and visually-pleasing appearance Nature presents, Her inherent influencing energies and their helpful and healing vibrations are the real gifts behind the external beauty we tend to perceive as Her complete totality.

FLOWERS

Alyssum
Symbology: inner balance and peace
Influencing energy: soothes emotions and encourages harmony

African Violet
Symbology: purity of thought and behavior
Influencing energy: promotes emotional healing

Amaryllis
Symbology: mental focus
Influencing energy: grounding force

Anemone
Symbology: mental awareness
Influencing energy: heightens perception; sharpens intellectual acuity

Angelica
Symbology: insight
Influencing energy: encourages clear thought

Apple blossom
Symbology: mental health
Influencing energy: cleanses mind of irrationality

Arnica
Symbology: priorities
Influencing energy: sustains goal determination

Aster
Symbology: memories
Influencing energy: inspires recall of important past experiences

Autumn leaves
Symbology: reflection
Influencing energy: promotes introspection/contemplation

Azalea
Symbology: hidden talents
Influencing energy: awakens recognition of one's unique abilities

Baby's breath
Symbology: rebirth; rejuvenation
Influencing energy: fosters emotional renewal

Bachelor's button
Symbology: self-reliance
Influencing energy: supports self-confidence and independence

Beardtongue
Symbology: humor
Influencing energy: uplifts general life outlook; promotes use of humor

Begonia
Symbology: emotional balance
Influencing energy: induces a sense of well-being

Bergamot
Symbology: a healing life aspect
Influencing energy: induces a recognition of those elements in one's life which have the potential to correct or ease difficult situations

Betony
Symbology: care needed for an emotional wound
Influencing energy: emotional healing element

Bird-of-paradise
Symbology: elaborate thoughts; extravagant ideas
Influencing energy: eases thoughts back down into reality

Bitterroot
Symbology: life difficulties
Influencing energy: strengthens perseverance

Bittersweet
Symbology: acceptance
Influencing energy: brings recognition of the fact that we must accept life rather than to buck it by attempting to go against that which is unalterable

Black-eyed Susan
Symbology: predictive of forthcoming favorable results
Influencing energy: provides encouragement; assurance

Black nightshade
Symbology: duality of human nature
Influencing energy: stimulates mental awareness

Blazing star
Symbology: inspiration
Influencing energy: opens one to new ideas and thought

Bleeding heart
Symbology: sympathy
Influencing energy: soothes sorrow/grief

Bluebell
Symbology: joy
Influencing energy: uplifts emotions

Bluebonnet
Symbology: aligned facets of an aspect
Influencing energy: highlights related elements of an issue or situation

Bougainvillea
Symbology: bright spiritual life
Influencing energy: stimulates one's beliefs

Buttercup
Symbology: inner happiness; laughter
Influencing energy: animation; induces the expression of joy

Camellia
Symbology: false beauty and/or innocence
Influencing energy: warns against pretense; induces a clear look at self

Candytuft
Symbology: joys; life's bright moments
Influencing energy: heightens appreciation of life's small blessings

Carnation
Symbology: social priorities
Influencing energy: aids in easing one's obsession with social mores

Cherry blossom
Symbology: a "sweet" situation; prime aspects
Influencing energy: endorses faith

Chicory
Symbology: alternatives
Influencing energy: clarifies recognition of alternatives and opportunities

Chrysanthemum
Symbology: a "golden time" of life
Influencing energy: deepens serenity

Cinquefoil
Symbology: light-heartedness
Influencing energy: encourages brighter outlook to life

Clematis
Symbology: the beautiful and prolific effects of acts of goodness which endure or "cling" to others
Influencing energy: enheartening effects; boosts sense of rightness

Coleus
Symbology: acceptance
Influencing energy: promotes tolerance of others

Columbine
Symbology: inner peacefulness
Influencing energy: fosters emotional tranquility

Comfrey
Symbology: acceptance
Influencing energy: restores one's inner balance

Coralroot
Symbology: spiritual qualities; compassion
Influencing energy: deepens emotional sensitivity toward others

Cornflower
Symbology: beauty of one's inner strength through self-reliance
Influencing energy: supports sense of self-confidence

Cowbane
Symbology: congeniality
Influencing energy: heightens perception of social interaction

Cowslip
Symbology: tranquility
Influencing energy: alleviates stress; calms emotionality

Crape myrtle
Symbology: synergy
Influencing energy: helps restore mental/emotional balance

Crocus
Symbology: marker for situational/directional change
Influencing energy: reinforces decisions

Daffodil
Symbology: bright prospects of new beginnings
Influencing energy: provides reassurance

Dahlia
Symbology: opportunities
Influencing energy: encouragement for one's self-confidence

Daisy
Symbology: emotional nourishment
Influencing energy: provides emotional uplift

Dandelion
Symbology: hidden qualities
Influencing energy: encourages one to look beyond the obvious in life

Datura
Symbology: life aspect which alters perspective, reaction, or comprehension
Influencing energy: skews reality into a false view

Day lily
Symbology: emotional sensitivity
Influencing energy: heightens emotional receptivity

Dogbane
Symbology: friendship
Influencing energy: magnifies value of close relationships

Dogwood
Symbology: beautiful beginnings
Influencing energy: induces faith in one's future

Edelweiss
Symbology: courage; tenacity
Influencing energy: upholds self-confidence and perseverance

Elecampane
Symbology: healing life element
Influencing energy: promotes emotional healing

Feverfew
Symbology: balance
Influencing energy: helps to unblock energy channels

Firethorn
Symbology: life's difficulties
Influencing energy: increases inner strength

Fireweed
Symbology: caution
Influencing energy: enhances perception of dangerous potentialities of life situations, relationships, or individuals

Flax

Symbology: opportunity

Influencing energy: fortifies recognition of the availability of different paths which offer opportunities

Fleabane

Symbology: defensive aspects which neutralize negative elements in one's life

Influencing energy: arouses faith in oneself

Forget-me-not

Symbology: specific need to remember something

Influencing energy: stimulates memory

Four-leaf clover

Symbology: potentiality; luck

Influencing energy: widens perceptual awareness of opportunity

Four-o-clock

Symbology: sheltering aspects; protective qualities

Influencing energy: strengthens self-confidence

Foxglove

Symbology: the healing abilities of one's natural talents

Influencing energy: reinforces inner strength

Frangipani

Symbology: emotional sensitivity

Influencing energy: stimulates empathy

Fuchsia

Symbology: compassion and love

Influencing energy: strengthens humanitarian sensitivities

Gardenia

Symbology: purity

Influencing energy: induces a less judgmental attitude

Gentian

Symbology: simplicity and innocence

Influencing energy: clarifies life priorities

Gentian violet
Symbology: the healing benefits of spiritual convictions
Influencing energy: instills greater faith in beliefs

Geranium
Symbology: optimism
Influencing energy: buoys one's outlook

Gladiolus
Symbology: joy
Influencing energy: intensifies an appreciation of life

Gloxinia
Symbology: deep inner joy
Influencing energy: externalizes happiness to others

Golden banner
Symbology: cheerfulness
Influencing energy: uplifts mood; promotes brighter perspective

Goldenrod
Symbology: natural talents
Influencing energy: emphasizes faith in the self as healer

Grape hyacinth
Symbology: the presence of many hidden abilities/talents
Influencing energy: impelling one to recognize that which is within self

Groundsel
Symbology: joy
Influencing energy: deepens appreciation of life's golden moments

Heliotrope
Symbology: inherent spiritual talents
Influencing energy: heightens the effectiveness of personal abilities

Hemlock
Symbology: an aspect containing positive and negative facets
Influencing energy: heightens perceptual awareness and judgement skills

Hepatica
Symbology: inner emotional strength
Influencing energy: provides the fortitude to persevere

Hibiscus
Symbology: spirituality
Influencing energy: promotes faith in beliefs

Hollyhock
Symbology: cheerfulness and bright outlook
Influencing energy: encourages the joy to be shared with others

Honeysuckle
Symbology: earned graces
Influencing energy: increases generosity

Hyacinth
Symbology: the blossoming of a new spiritual gift
Influencing energy: fosters development

Hydrangea
Symbology: generous utilization of one's humanitarianism
Influencing energy: enhances fulfillment

Impatiens
Symbology: frequent moments of joy
Influencing energy: deepens appreciation of life

Indian blanket
Symbology: protective aspects
Influencing energy: reinforces one's inner defenses; deepens confidence

Indian paintbrush
Symbology: vibrant emotional/spiritual energy
Influencing energy: encourages recognition of blessings

Iris
Symbology: hope
Influencing energy: incentive to persevere

Jack-in-the-pulpit
Symbology: broadens emotional/spiritual expressiveness
Influencing energy: increased effectiveness upon others

Jacob's ladder
Symbology: a delicate situation; a fragile relationship
Influencing energy: heightens perceptual sensitivity

Jasmine
Symbology: mysterious quality to personality
Influencing energy: increases magnetism

Jonquil
Symbology: peacefulness
Influencing energy: enhances tranquility within self and upon others

Knapweed
Symbology: emotional stability
Influencing energy: promotes emotional balance

Lady's slipper
Symbology: fragile natural talents which need nurturing
Influencing energy: reinforces/strengthens talents

Larkspur
Symbology: talents generously shared
Influencing energy: instills faith in others

Laurel
Symbology: gentleness
Influencing energy: promotes emotional sensitivity

Lavender
Symbology: gentleness; a comforting spiritual belief
Influencing energy: increases peace of mind

Lilac
Symbology: spiritual purity
Influencing energy: prompting increased spiritual wisdom; enhances love

Lily
Symbology: innocence and purity; new birth
Influencing energy: inducing emotional respite; tranquility

Lily of the valley
Symbology: naivete; lack of worldly experience
Influencing energy: fosters a sense of solace in simplicity

Lobelia
Symbology: an emotionally calming life aspect
Influencing energy: enhances serenity

Locoweed
Symbology: presence of a polarized aspect in one's life
Influencing energy: stimulates awareness of a situational duality

Lotus
Symbology: spiritual sacredness
Influencing energy: promotes a deeper appreciation of beliefs

Lousewort
Symbology: irritations in life; life's difficulties
Influencing energy: encourages perseverance

Lupine
Symbology: longevity
Influencing energy: invigorates flow of inner balance

Magnolia
Symbology: the fragile and delicate aspects in one's life
Influencing energy: deepens the desire to cherish these aspects

Mallow
Symbology: broad scope natural talents
Influencing energy: stimulates the growth of these talents by way of sharing

Marigold
Symbology: encouragement
Influencing energy: deepens sense of reassurance

Mariposa lily
Symbology: hope
Influencing energy: counters urge to give up

Marsh marigold
Symbology: spiritual encouragement
Influencing energy: invigorates one's faith in personal belief systems

Meadowsweet
Symbology: serenity
Influencing energy: augments acceptance; rekindles tolerance

Milkweed
Symbology: emotional sustenance
Influencing energy: elevates emotional level; eases depression

Mimosa
Symbology: a delicate innocence of character, fragile yet strong
Influencing energy: maintains the fine balance of innocence and strength

Mock orange
Symbology: brighter perspectives; refreshing viewpoints
Influencing energy: raises and expands outlook

Monkey-flower
Symbology: carefree personality
Influencing energy: tends to remind one of the need to stay grounded

Monkshood
Symbology: a dangerous or negative situation
Influencing energy: increases awareness

Moonflower

Symbology: blossoming wisdom

Influencing energy: advocates caution in the way of being analytical

Morning glory

Symbology: emotional/spiritual expression

Influencing energy: strengthens incentive to be open with feelings

Mullein

Symbology: healing aspects in life

Influencing energy: promotes well-being

Myrtle

Symbology: gentleness

Influencing energy: protection from any tendency to be harsh

Narcissus

Symbology: dangers of egotism

Influencing energy: promotes awareness of others

Nasturtium

Symbology: fulfillment through utilization of talents

Influencing energy: instills encouragement

Oleander

Symbology: represents a dangerous life aspect

Influencing energy: heightens watchfulness

Orchid

Symbology: fragile talent or benefit which must be carefully utilized

Influencing energy: brings an understanding that fragility doesn't also mean weakness or powerlessness

Pansy

Symbology: fearful personality; fear of ridicule or reprisal

Influencing energy: stimulates self-confidence

Parsley

Symbology: hidden opportunities

Influencing energy: sharpens recognition of advantageous life aspects

Pasqueflower

Symbology: spiritual inspiration

Influencing energy: motivates one to delve into deeper spiritual concepts

Passion flower

Symbology: the beauty of the passion of empathy/compassion

Influencing energy: induces heightened sensitivity

Pennyroyal

Symbology: purification

Influencing energy: helps to alleviate negative attitudes

Penstemon

Symbology: interconnectedness; life's relatedness

Influencing energy: helps to intensify sensitivity to all aspects of life

Peony

Symbology: emotional sensitivity

Influencing energy: amplifying emotional protection

Periwinkle

Symbology: fragile talent; inherent ability

Influencing energy: stimulates desire to utilize talents/abilities

Petunia

Symbology: a talent or ability which will proliferate if cared for

Influencing energy: inducement to appreciate and tend to talents

Phlox

Symbology: cheerfulness

Influencing energy: uplifts mood

Poinsettia

Symbology: externalized spiritual self-expression; spiritual celebration

Influencing energy: advocates joy taken in one's beliefs

Poppy

Symbology: a natural talent having positive/negative elements depending on its specific utilization

Influencing energy: promotes an awareness of life's duality

Primrose

Symbology: an ideal of perfection; a cure-all element

Influencing energy: dispels misconceptions

Purple coneflower

Symbology: intense healing aspect in life

Influencing energy: reinforces inner strength and fortitude

Pussytoes

Symbology: gentleness

Influencing energy: helps to alleviate personality harshness

Queen Anne's lace

Symbology: a life facet containing positive and negative aspects

Influencing energy: clarifies the existence of duality

Rabbitbrush

Symbology: personal defenses

Influencing energy: bestows inner strength

Ragwort

Symbology: introspection

Influencing energy: stimulates contemplation

Red raspberry

Symbology: cleansing element

Influencing energy: aids in ridding self of negativity

Red clover

Symbology: strong inner strength

Influencing energy: instills recognition of personal defenses

Redroot

Symbology: perceptual clarity

Influencing energy: helps to clear away emotional blocks to rationale

Rhododendron

Symbology: a source of bountiful natural elements

Influencing energy: encourages awareness of one's capability to be a wellspring of blessings to others; opens the door to recognition of one's inner goodness and opportunities to utilize same

Rose

Symbology: strong admiration

Influencing energy: transmits emotional attitudes; enheartening qualities

Sage

Symbology: purification

Influencing energy: stimulates a desire to rid self of negativity

Salsify

Symbology: mental focus

Influencing energy: sharpens one's perspective of priority

Sand lily

Symbology: life's smaller blessings

Influencing energy: heightens appreciation of the little aspects which brighten life

Saxifrage

Symbology: meaningful moments; valuable times

Influencing energy: sharpens recognition of important life aspects

Scullcap

Symbology: inspiration

Influencing energy: enhances new thought; widens perceptual abilities

Shepherd's purse
Symbology: thoughtfulness
Influencing energy: amplifies thoughts toward others; reduces self-centeredness

Shooting star
Symbology: individuality
Influencing energy: strengthens one's appreciation of individuality

Snakeweed
Symbology: mental acuity
Influencing energy: sharpens perception and awareness

Snapdragon
Symbology: secretiveness; ability to hold one's tongue
Influencing energy: enhances trust and integrity

Snowberry
Symbology: perceptual awareness
Influencing energy: helps to heighten one's awareness

Snow-on-the-mountain
Symbology: developing talents
Influencing energy: raises awareness of personal skills and the perception of the multitude ways to actuate them

Soapwort
Symbology: cleansing
Influencing energy: helps alleviate negative attitudes

Solomon's seal
Symbology: rationale; justice
Influencing energy: increases analytical skill

Spring beauty
Symbology: renewal
Influencing energy: encourages brighter perspectives; rejuvenates

Starwort
Symbology: priorities
Influencing energy: enhances perception of life's more valuable facets

Statice

Symbology: endurance

Influencing energy: empowers self-confidence; strengthens perseverance

Stonecrop

Symbology: destiny

Influencing energy: empowers the strength of acceptance in one's life

Sunflower

Symbology: spiritual joy

Influencing energy: underscores one's blessings and appreciation of same

Sweet clover

Symbology: emotional sensitivity

Influencing energy: enriches emotional perception

Sweet pea

Symbology: delicate, fragile aspects

Influencing energy: encourages sensitivity to delicate relationships or situations

Tansy

Symbology: protection

Influencing energy: reinforces one's inherent defensive qualities; strengthens insight

Thimbleberry

Symbology: details

Influencing energy: heightens analytical attention

Thistle

Symbology: life lessons

Influencing energy: magnifies one's ability to recognize value of experiences

Trumpet flower

Symbology: spiritual message

Influencing energy: an inducement to share spiritual concepts

Tulip
Symbology: encouragement
Influencing energy: raises self-confidence; instills sense of support

Twinflower
Symbology: duality
Influencing energy: helps to recognize multitude of facets of a situation, relationship or individual

Valerian
Symbology: tranquility
Influencing energy: assists in alleviating stress

Verbena
Symbology: life's blessings
Influencing energy: prompts recognition of life's positive facets

Violet
Symbology: spiritual facets associated with a life aspect
Influencing energy: widens overall perspective

Wallflower
Symbology: hidden qualities
Influencing energy: helps to expose and highlight one's admirable traits

Water lily
Symbology: spiritual beauty
Influencing energy: a sense of spiritual serenity

Wintergreen
Symbology: renewal; new facets to an aspect
Influencing energy: widens perspective

Wisteria
Symbology: spiritual grace
Influencing energy: instills tranquility into one's nature

Wood lily
Symbology: rejuvenation
Influencing energy: stimulates determination; instills encouragement

Wood sorrel
Symbology: encouragement
Influencing energy: strengthens resolve and self-confidence

Yampa
Symbology: delicate situation or relationship
Influencing energy: heightens one's sense of diplomacy

Yarrow
Symbology: independence
Influencing energy: reinforces confidence in one's self-sufficiency

Yucca
Symbology: cleansing element
Influencing energy: tends to bring clarity regarding complex idea/concepts

Zinnia
Symbology: multiple benefits or gifts in one's life which have not yet been recognized
Influencing energy: increases awareness and discernment

QUESTIONS ABOUT FLOWERS

Do flowers have to be growing in order to be effective?

What this correspondent means is whether flowers have to be rooted in a garden or pot, as opposed to cut flowers in order to be effective. The answer is no because the flower still contains its basic essence whether it's rooted or cut. The only difference is that a rooted flower will, of course, last longer.

Are dried flowers effective?

Sure they are. We not only dry flowers to preserve their physical beauty, they're dried to also preserve their essence.

Is flower incense good to burn?

Flower incense, if true to the original fragrance, will emanate the same type of energy influence as if you were growing the blossoms in your home.

Do oils made from the flower have potency?

Oils made from flowers may actually increase the potency of the blossom's specific influencing energy. Use caution when using strong concentrations of oils.

Are local flowers more beneficial than those gathered from another locale?

No, because the flowers themselves contain their own inherent energies which are generated from their composition, not from those of the soil they grew in.

Do flowers emanate two kinds of influences, a psychosomatic one and a physiological one?

Most of them do, although not all flower essences used in the methodologies of aromatherapy and homeopathy will be utilized for the same purposes.

My neighbor thinks I'm some dark alchemist because I make oils and infusions from flowers. Comment?

You don't need me to comment on this. You know that her opinion is based on ignorance, so why let it bother you? Grandmother Earth is the greatest alchemist of all. She provides us with everything we need for treating our psychological and physical conditions. If your neighbor has a garden, or buys flats of flowers in the spring to plant, or allows cut flowers in her home, then she's being somewhat contradictory without realizing it. Flowers, no matter what form they take, whether they're in the form of fresh blossoms, oils, dried mementos, or perfume, are gifts from Grandmother Earth.

I have a pendant made of a rose bud enclosed in lucite. Does this emit energy from the flower?

No, because the energy is encapsulated within the smothering composition of the lucite. This is not to say that the flower no longer possesses energy, it is merely confined.

What portion of a flower contains the most potent percent of its energy?

In most cases, it's the blossom. With some species it's the leaf.

TREES

Acacia
Symbology: multifaceted element; complexity
Influencing energy: clarifies, simplifies ideas and concepts

Alder
Symbology: cherished moments
Influencing energy: enhances emotional impact of heartfelt moments; appreciation

Almond
Symbology: need to avoid stress
Influencing energy: relieves tension and effects of same

Apple
Symbology: good health
Influencing energy: helps to shift one's focus to healthful life elements

Apricot
Symbology: healing force
Influencing energy: strengthens immune system; reinforces self-healing energies

Ash
Symbology: need to de-emphasize physical aspects
Influencing energy: lessens materialistic attitude

Aspen
Symbology: compassion
Influencing energy: heightens sensitivity to others; shifts focus from self

Avocado
Symbology: optimism
Influencing energy: enhances perspective, outlook

Balsa
Symbology: talents and thoughts which lighten burdens
Influencing energy: inspires creative solutions

Balsam
Symbology: spiritual serenity
Influencing energy: deepens personal spiritual fulfillment

Bamboo
Symbology: developing talents
Influencing energy: clarifies need for linear advancement in proper stages

Banana
Symbology: hidden resources
Influencing energy: sharpens recognition of the more subtle values in life

Basswood
Symbology: strength
Influencing energy: fortifies determination

Bayberry
Symbology: reminiscing; remembrances
Influencing energy: sparks insight from memories

Beech
Symbology: palatable lessons experienced
Influencing energy: deepens one's level of acceptance

Birch
Symbology: honest and open situation or atmosphere
Influencing energy: assists in defining separate aspects to an element

Bitternut
Symbology: hard lessons in life
Influencing energy: promotes deeper understanding and acceptance of experiential tribulations and difficulties

Bittersweet
Symbology: duality
Influencing energy: reminds us that beauty and positive aspects often follow on the heels of emotional pain

Black haw

Symbology: rewards; recompense

Influencing energy: helps to highlight life's blessings and the positive elements resulting from our acts of goodness

Black locust

Symbology: assuredness

Influencing energy: fortifies self-confidence; trust in self

Black oak

Symbology: strong negative aspect in one's life

Influencing energy: assists in defining one's behavioral areas which need correction

Black walnut

Symbology: fruit of one's labors

Influencing energy: intensifies personal fulfillment resulting from hard work

Blue spruce

Symbology: connectedness to spirituality through nature

Influencing energy: heightens one's spiritual relatedness to all of life

Bonsai

Symbology: forced attitudes; mental manipulation

Influencing energy: promotes self-discovery, revelation; helps to reveal true motives

Boxelder

Symbology: courage

Influencing energy: supportive; encourages self-confidence

Breadfruit

Symbology: encouragement

Influencing energy: stimulates self-confidence

Buckthorn

Symbology: achievements

Influencing energy: helps to center one's focus on goals

Butternut

Symbology: congeniality

Influencing energy: broadens range of receptivity to others

Bristlecone pine

Symbology: lessons in life

Influencing energy: strengthens resolve to learn from mistakes

Cajeput

Symbology: impetus; stimulation

Influencing energy: bestows sense of encouragement

Catalpa

Symbology: priorities

Influencing energy: helps to highlight important aspects of one's life

Cedar

Symbology: energized protection of one's spiritual beliefs

Influencing energy: increases spiritual conviction

Cherry

Symbology: "sweet" situation; prime aspects

Influencing energy: heightens awareness of prime opportunities

Chestnut

Symbology: warm emotions; heartfelt feelings

Influencing energy: intensifies emotional depth

Chicory

Symbology: "substitute" for strength and motivation

Influencing energy: increases recognition of life alternatives

Chinaberry

Symbology: sensitivity

Influencing energy: brings an awareness to delicate situations

Chokecherry
Symbology: sorrowful life aspects
Influencing energy: eases grief; heightens acceptance

Christmas berry
Symbology: spiritual joy
Influencing energy: deepens faith

Cocoa
Symbology: soothing aspect in life
Influencing energy: encourages utilization of helpful life elements

Coconut palm
Symbology: strength/nourishment from hard lessons
Influencing energy: increases understanding; deepens inner strength

Coffee tree
Symbology: impetus; energizing element
Influencing energy: stimulates motivation

Coralbean
Symbology: multifaceted aspects to an element
Influencing energy: helps to bring clarity to a complex or cloudy situation

Cork
Symbology: multilevel abilities
Influencing energy: reveals wider range of options for talent utilization

Cottonwood
Symbology: beauty of combining wholesome living with spirituality
Influencing energy: intensifies one's "living" of beliefs

Crab Apple
Symbology: "tart" personality or situation
Influencing energy: helps to expose sensitive relationships or situations

Cucumber tree
Symbology: lasting effects; results
Influencing energy: emphasizes effects of one's actions

Cypress
Symbology: grief; a mourning time
Influencing energy: soothes sorrow

Dogwood
Symbology: beautiful beginnings
Influencing energy: promotes bright perspectives

Douglas fir
Symbology: cherished spiritual beliefs or living philosophy
Influencing energy: amplifies convictions

Ebony
Symbology: enduring puzzlement
Influencing energy: pinpoints areas of comprehension difficulties to clarify

Elderberry
Symbology: naturally-occurring opportunities often overlooked
Influencing energy: sharpens one's awareness of potentiality

Elm
Symbology: escapism
Influencing energy: encourages one to face life; gives inner strength

Engelmann spruce
Symbology: perseverance; fortitude; hardiness
Influencing energy: instills courage and forbearance

English walnut
Symbology: richly nourishing aspect in one's life
Influencing energy: heightens appreciation of life's gifts

Eucalyptus
Symbology: life aspect capable of nourishing through a healing
Influencing energy: serves to clear out psychological blocks

Fig

Symbology: inner nourishment

Influencing energy: fortifies self-confidence; encouragement

Fringe tree

Symbology: peripheral elements; hidden aspects

Influencing energy: disclosure; aids in exposing all facets to an element

Giant sequoia

Symbology: ancient truths which remain immutable

Influencing energy: deepens conviction regarding personal and unique philosophical concepts

Ginkgo

Symbology: memories; remembrance

Influencing energy: instills a sense of importance to certain experiences

Hackberry

Symbology: discernment

Influencing energy: sharpens analytical thought

Hawthorn

Symbology: unrecognized benefits

Influencing energy: increases awareness of opportunities and widens perception of additional aspects to an element

Hazelnut

Symbology: common sense

Influencing energy: increases accuracy of one's rationale

Hemlock

Symbology: dangerous factors in one's life; an element containing duality

Influencing energy: assists in comprehending the positive aspects to a seemingly negative element

Hickory

Symbology: strength and enduring characteristics of one's natural abilities as they're developed and utilized

Influencing energy: fosters an appreciation of one's personal helpfulness

Holly

Symbology: fresh spiritual idea or insight

Influencing energy: inspires epiphanies

Honey locust

Symbology: results; conclusions

Influencing energy: clarifies methods of resolution

Horsechestnut

Symbology: inner strength; determination

Influencing energy: reinforces resolve

Ironwood

Symbology: complexity; intricate elements

Influencing energy: helps to separate out multilevel facets to a situation or relationship

Jamaica caper

Symbology: enriching life elements

Influencing energy: deepens appreciation

Joshua tree

Symbology: multiple positive facets to an element

Influencing energy: heightens recognition of blessings; increases recognition of all beneficial aspects to a situation, condition, or relationship

Juniper

Symbology: spiritual sustenance

Influencing energy: enriches nourishment, fulfillment from spiritual beliefs

Larch

Symbology: state of fragile balance one has caused talents to be in

Influencing energy: strengthens effectiveness of abilities

Lilac
Symbology: spiritual purity
Influencing energy: promotes increased spiritual wisdom; enhances depth of love

Lodgepole pine
Symbology: spiritual tenacity
Influencing energy: fosters serenity through confidence in spiritual beliefs

Macadamia
Symbology: psychological nourishment
Influencing energy: enriches emotional responsiveness

Magnolia
Symbology: fragile or delicate aspect in one's life
Influencing energy: deepens the desire to cherish these aspects

Mahogany
Symbology: strength
Influencing energy: supports self-confidence, assuredness

Mango
Symbology: hardened external personality covering inner sensitivity
Influencing energy: eases one's sensitivity into confidence of expression

Mangrove
Symbology: spiritual bounties; multiple blessings
Influencing energy: enhances awareness of life's many gifts

Manzanita
Symbology: cleansing qualities
Influencing energy: assists one in making corrections to the small personal frailties

Maple
Symbology: fruits of one's labors
Influencing energy: encourages a contentedness in laboring for needs and goals

Mescal bean
Symbology: irrationality; lack of reason
Influencing energy: stabilizes rationale; grounds thought process

Mesquite
Symbology: potent spiritual force; exceptional strength of spiritual knowledge and/or wisdom
Influencing energy: enhances spiritual potentiality

Mock orange
Symbology: contentedness
Influencing energy: deepens personal serenity

Monkey puzzle
Symbology: complexities; complications
Influencing energy: helps to bring clarity to complicated situations

Mulberry
Symbology: joy
Influencing energy: magnifies inner happiness

Norfolk Island pine
Symbology: emotional fragility
Influencing energy: heightens sensitivity to others

Nutmeg hickory
Symbology: cherished memories
Influencing energy: maintains strong emotional associations to past events one wishes to hold close to the heart

Oak
Symbology: unyielding personality; lack of spirituality
Influencing energy: stimulates sensitivity responsiveness

Olive
Symbology: beneficial element in one's life
Influencing energy: increases an awareness of positive life facets

Orange
Symbology: nourishing benefits from utilizing inner energies for benefit of others
Influencing energy: augments receptivity of positive elements

Palm
Symbology: spiritual freedom
Influencing energy: empowers and supports one's spiritual convictions

Papaya
Symbology: stress; anxiety; emotionalism
Influencing energy: somewhat tranquilizing; calms hypersensitivity

Pawpaw
Symbology: subtle effects; hidden positive facets to an element
Influencing energy: sharpens awareness of subtleties

Peach
Symbology: satisfaction; a desired result or element
Influencing energy: deepens trust in self and one's decisions

Pear
Symbology: duality
Influencing energy: sharpens observational skills

Pecan
Symbology: fulfillment
Influencing energy: deepens sense of reward after achievement

Pepper tree
Symbology: acceptance
Influencing energy: encourages acceptance; levels out emotional range

Persimmon
Symbology: enduring puzzlement
Influencing energy: helps to unravel confoundments; clarifies resolutions

Pine

Symbology: natural abilities; one's bonded relationship with nature

Influencing energy: enhances sense of interconnectedness to all of life

Pinyon pine

Symbology: fruits of our labor

Influencing energy: encourages self-reliance

Pistachio

Symbology: soothing element

Influencing energy: tends to ease irritation

Plum

Symbology: element of high quality in one's life

Influencing energy: reinforces ability to recognize life's blessings

Poison sumac

Symbology: dangerous ground

Influencing energy: assists in sharpening foresight, instincts

Poisontree

Symbology: a dangerous element

Influencing energy: hones perception, awareness

Poplar

Symbology: personal talent which has grown in an accelerated manner

Influencing energy: enriches appreciation for gifts of ability

Prickly ash

Symbology: tolerance

Influencing energy: reinforces attitude of acceptance

Redbud

Symbology: personality fragility

Influencing energy: strengthens level of emotional sensitivity

Redwood
Symbology: inner strength; fortitude
Influencing energy: supports perseverance

Rosewood
Symbology: an enduring natural talent or ability
Influencing energy: extends potency of an ability through a recognition of opportunity for utilization

Rubber
Symbology: tolerance
Influencing energy: encourages acceptance

Russian Olive
Symbology: spiritual elements; peaceful aspects
Influencing energy: helps to give greater notice to life's spiritual facets; aids in raising awareness to observe the beauty and goodness in life

Sandalwood
Symbology: unaffected personality
Influencing energy: instills sense of individuality

Sassafras
Symbology: well-being
Influencing energy: aids in increasing self-confidence and brightening perspective

Saw palmetto
Symbology: spiritual freedom
Influencing energy: supplements one's sense to believe in unique and personal philosophical concepts

Sea grape
Symbology: fruitful efforts
Influencing energy: restores faith in self

Serviceberry
Symbology: opportunity
Influencing energy: advocates awareness of options

Silktree
Symbology: delicate situation/relationship
Influencing energy: heightens sensitivity to others

Silver bell
Symbology: awareness
Influencing energy: increases observational skills

Slippery elm
Symbology: a healing element in one's life
Influencing energy: empowers self-correction; helps to understand that one has the ability to help self, make adjustments to new situations

Smokethorn
Symbology: spiritual depth, wisdom
Influencing energy: deepens wisdom of spiritual philosophy in relation to reality and the Divine Consciousness

Soapberry
Symbology: clearing out; cleansing
Influencing energy: improves energy (chi) circulation; helps to dissipate psychological blocks

Sourwood
Symbology: acceptance
Influencing energy: lessens attitude of intolerance

Spicewood
Symbology: spiritual talents/gifts
Influencing energy: emphasizes one's inner spiritual beauty

Sugarberry
Symbology: attained goals
Influencing energy: enriches fulfillment of achieved plans

Sugar maple
Symbology: serenity from wisdom
Influencing energy: enhances an awareness of tranquility related to spiritual wisdom

Sumac
Symbology: opportunity
Influencing energy: heightens recognition of options and available paths

Sweet bay
Symbology: rewards; benefits of independence
Influencing energy: boosts self-confidence and self-reliance

Sweet gum
Symbology: an enriching element in one's life
Influencing energy: enhances appreciation and fulfillment of positive aspects and blessings

Sycamore
Symbology: romance; admiration
Influencing energy: deepens emotional responses

Tallowwood
Symbology: enlightenment; perspective clarity
Influencing energy: sharpens perceptual acuity

Tamarack
Symbology: spiritual fragility
Influencing energy: fortifies fragile spiritual elements in one's life

Tupelo
Symbology: insight
Influencing energy: broadens perspective; deepens analytical thought

Vanilla
Symbology: renewal
Influencing energy: stimulates positive perspective; a view to the brighter side

Wahoo
Symbology: spiritual fulfillment
Influencing energy: deepens convictions

Weeping willow
Symbology: beauty and sensitivity of nature
Influencing energy: heightens nature awareness; inspires wisdom from nature observations

Willow
Symbology: spiritual tenacity and attraction
Influencing energy: empowers perseverance to achieve spiritual maturity

Winterberry
Symbology: spiritual isolation
Influencing energy: intensifies solace in spiritual beliefs

Witch Hazel
Symbology: a healing life aspect
Influencing energy: enhances effects of inner healing forces

Yellowwood
Symbology: fruits of one's labor
Influencing energy: compels advancement; stimulates desire to persevere

QUESTIONS ABOUT TREES

What makes a forest feel so wonderfully fresh and invigorating, yet the deep woods feel ominous and spooky?

First of all, we need to clarify that the forest (deep or otherwise) feels wonderfully fresh and invigorating because it *is* fresh and invigorating. By its very nature it's re-oxygenating the very air you breathe. The pine scent is fresh and wonderful to breathe in and fill your lungs with. Its bare beingness is pure innocence and is there to provide you with serenity and peace. Those deep woods you seem to be so anxious about are the same as the "lighter" forests you love, only more intense.

That energy intensity can oftentimes seem overpowering and frequently misinterpreted as threatening. Those woods are also thriving with wildlife which many folks are unfamiliar with. These create a sense of being on foreign soil—out of one's known environment—and, therefore, one can experience a lack of trust and self-confidence associated with this. As many years as I've lived in and around forests, I'm still amazed at the wide variety of woodsy "people" occupying them.

Around my wooded cabin, the forest teems with life. Raccoons come to eat every night on my porch, deer come in separate family groups to enjoy the sweet feed grain I keep out, a mama black bear comes with her cub to clean up whatever the others have left and drink from the birdbath, and all day long the place is like a bird sanctuary with the trees and porch feeders filled with dozens of varieties of feathered people, including soaring redtail hawks. Coyotes have worn a criss-crossed trail over my drive and they routinely romp and hunt down in the valley below my cabin. When driving down my drive, which winds through a quarter mile of heavy woods, I'll spot ermine, badgers, foxes, rabbits, and other critters' eyes reflected in the headlights. During a woodswalk a bobcat or cougar might be sighted. Sitting out in the woods in the afternoon, the underbrush seems to be always moving somewhere near. In the forest you're never alone. There are always eyes watching you. Yet this knowledge doesn't equate to fear or "spookiness" of any kind. It's not in the least "ominous" or scary . . . it's natural. Just natural nature. Our cities and houses insulate people from the beautiful, free expression of nature at its best. The sights, sounds, and scents of the deep woods create a soothing backdrop for the continuing drama which is played out upon its pinecone-studded stage.

Ominous? No, magnanimous. The woods are full of eyes watching you. The forests are alive with silent watchers and, unless you too become a watcher, you'll forever remain an outsider who is fearful of reaching out to touch the soul of nature.

Does driftwood give any influence?

Driftwood still has composition. That composition is unique unto the specific species of tree it came from, therefore, it maintains its natural influential energy. Sometimes, seeing deadwood, we're struck with the initial impression that it's completely benign—dead—but that's not so. Everything has cellular makeup and energy. Everything in nature has influence.

Will woodcarvings of an identical figure give off different energies if they're made from various species of wood?

Certainly. If identical images of a Buddha were carved out of applewood, aspen, ironwood, and maple they'd all have different influences generated from their unique composition and the energies those emanate. The shape of, or what man does to, that wood does not alter its inherent cellular structure.

I love to decorate with bittersweet but sometimes it makes me feel sad. Why?

The wood of bittersweet is somewhat tortured, in that it's twisted and bent. It represents acceptance and its energies urge us to accept life rather than to continually fight it by going against the grain. Bittersweet says, "Reality *is*. Accept it. Recognize your life blessings and cherish them, while also accepting life's bumps and bruises." Bittersweet says, "Ride the flowing current of reality." Perhaps it makes you feel sad because you're centering on the bumps and bruises too much. Bittersweet is duality. It's the duality of positive and negative forces associated with an element. It's the balanced scale of life whereby the good and bad facets are kept on a finely calibrated measurement which maintains our perceptual equilibrium.

What makes a mature blue spruce seem so majestic?

That's one of its innate qualities, isn't it? A tall and full blue spruce will tower high into the sky and reach its branches wide and far. Its color brings to mind a sense of "freshness" of life and it sends out a wonderfully pleasing fragrance. Although these characteristics alone would make one think of majesty, its true splendor comes from the multitude of lives which thrive within its branches. I have an enormous blue spruce living beside my front porch and, to me, I see this tree as being likened to an entire city housing a whole society of little, feathered people. Its branches are loaded with all kinds of nests. This particular blue spruce is like a mother with her arms sheltering all her infants. I think that, sometimes, we "see" things and don't "observe" them. From the "seeing" we get impressions such as majesty, but only after true observation of them do we come to understand the reason behind the initial sense of character.

In your book, Fireside, *you were burning High Mountain Cedar incense throughout the entire evening's conversation. Any particular reason why that particular scent? Do you burn any other variety?*

I burn the High Mountain Cedar because it has a strong cedar scent which fills the entire cabin. This cedar is a "match" for me. By that I mean that it perfectly aligns with my beingness, my vibrations. Therefore, it provides a deep sense of serenity within me. It's me. There are two more types of incense fragrance I burn. One is the Number 2 Gnosh Sticks brand of *Oils and Spices*, which manifests a homey reminiscence of an ancient lifetime; the second is the Fred Soll brand of *Desert Patchouli* which also aligns with my energies. These three are the only incense fragrances I burn. Even the only perfume I wear is formulated from a blend of patchouli, frankincense, and orange.

Which part of the eucalyptus tree is more potent, the leaves or the wood?

Though the leaves contain the fragrance, the wood is that part which produced those leaves. The wood holds more potent influential energy than the leaves.

Does petrified wood still retain its original influence?

This question is much like the petrified wood one in the section on gemstones. Yes, although the wood's appearance has altered, it still retains its influential energy. It is still composed of its original cellular matter.

Ironwood is so beautiful when carved and polished, but doesn't it have an extremely heavy or dense vibration?

That's an assumption and false impression based on visual attributes. Yes, ironwood is extremely dense, but dense doesn't necessarily equate to vibrational heaviness. Rather than being heavy, or giving the sense of confusing, problematical elements, it manages to influence the direct opposite—it *clarifies* complexities.

Do trees which grow along watercourses give off more spiritual energies than trees growing elsewhere?

Somewhat. I say "somewhat" because their inherent composition *takes on* a certain amount of spiritual influence from its surroundings which, in this case, would be the water. The tree's makeup absorbs this influence within its very cellular structure, thereby incorporating spiritual aspects to its basic composition.

Are giant sequoias meant to remind us of our proper place on the planet?

Not specifically, but they certainly do make us feel diminutive, don't they? They stand for "ancient truths," the immutable "solid" aspects of reality which remain unchanged throughout time and are completely unaffected by the existence of or the effects of the human hand or mind. Perhaps it is this influence which diminishes our self-perspective. Perhaps it is that we subconsciously realize that there is something of nature on this planet that is far greater and more stupendous than we are.

The sugar maple is so brilliant in the autumn sun, it seems as though it was meant to be some sign to people. Am I way off base here?

Like the former question, this is evidence of how effectively nature affects us. No, you're not way off base with this, but the sugar maple wasn't specifically "meant" to be some type of sign; it just inspires such on its own, through our acute observation of nature in conjunction with our spiritually philosophical mind. To a person who is accustomed to deep thought, the observance of nature heightens wonder. It gives validating credence to higher thought and spiritual perception. To notice a wildflower and be awe-struck at its beauty, as the lowering sun backlights its tiny petal veins, is to sense one's connection to that simple fragrant life. To contemplate whether or not that blazing, sun-touched sugar maple was meant as a sign to humankind is to understand our true relatedness with all of life. You see, it's not the tree doing the communicating, it's you! You are recognizing your presence which is a vitally alive thread upon the great Web of Life. Your thread connected to your neighbor's, which is connected to the deer's, the tree's, the butterfly's, the hills, and the valleys. Every thread having energy of consciousness. Every thread communicating.

Does the clear-cutting of trees have a negative effect on the remaining forest?

Sure it does. All living things have consciousness (energy) and that consciousness is what makes up the great Web of Life. Interconnectedness. Relatedness. All of life is intricately intertwined. Every action creates a reactive effect on something else. We are not a planet of "ones," we are a planet of many comprising "one consciousness."

What makes sandalwood such a popular choice for incense?

The general answer to that would be because it simply smells good, it's a pleasing fragrance. To expand on this would be to make assumptions because everyone is different and will choose sandalwood for equally different reasons.

I know witch-hazel is wonderful for cleansing and as an astringent; does it do anything else?

Other than the external, physical healing influences which its energies emanate, it also reinforces and bolsters the inner healing forces of self, the body's immune system. Its effects are of a strengthening nature which speeds cellular reaction time.

The weeping willow has such a sorrowful, melancholy appearance. Is this external characteristic reflective of its natural energy influence?

No. You're transferring a personal, emotional attitude to a facet of nature. Although the weeping willow may seem melancholy, its true nature is more of an inherent "sensitivity," thus you see the fragile gracefulness and misinterpret it as sadness. This tree symbolizes the beauty and sensitivity of nature and its influencing energy heightens an awareness of nature itself. It aids in inspiring wisdom gained from the observations of nature.

Regarding holly, are the leaves or the wood more potent?

In the case of holly, the leaves contain an amount of influencing energy equal to the wood they grow out from. Holly is a highly potent species.

Why is bayberry a candle scent commonly associated with Christmas?

I don't think there's any official history connecting bayberry to this holiday yet it would seem to be a logical choice of scent because of the winter season Christmas falls in. Because of the Christmas "tree," we associate the holiday with woodsy things like holly, pine boughs, the yule log, and forest fragrances. Bayberry is a forest fragrance and brings the mind to thoughts reminiscent of Christmases past. Bayberry symbolizes "remembrances" and its energy tends to empower recall of these past memories whereby we gain insight and wisdom from reviewing them. Christmastide is a unique time for creating lasting memories and bayberry is a highly influential force for imprinting those memories upon the mind.

Do willows carry energy of a spiritual nature due to the location they grow in?

Sure, because they grow along watercourses and water symbolizes spiritual aspects in life. Like the cottonwood, trees which thrive near water absorb the water's influence within their cellular structure where it becomes an innate component of its makeup. The willow symbolizes the attraction of spiritual elements in life and the resulting tenacity for gaining spiritual knowledge. It strengthens one's perseverance to gain spiritual maturity.

What about woodburning? When we burn wood in our fireplaces and woodstoves, are the energies destroyed or released?

They can't be destroyed because energy is ongoing. The wood's influence is released in the heat and smoke, it maintains its viability within the remaining ashes. When I clean out my woodstove I let the ashes sit in a container outside until they're cold then disperse them in the woods to nourish the forest floor. In this manner the tree's cycle of life is taken full circle.

Life from Her Whispered Breath

The Earth's Grandmother Spirit is the life force of the planet. From Her gentle and sweet breath She breathes vitality into the thriving multitudes of those people who heavily populate the earth, air, and water. Some of these furred, feathered, and finned people have willingly shared their energy influences with humans from the beginning of time. They are a vital facet of every strand contained within the Great Web of Life. Some indigenous culture lores refer to these special helpful forces as "totems," yct to infer that these narrowly selected totem groups are all-inclusive would be to do a serious disservice to the composite civilization of critter people who co-habit this reality with us. The current conceptual idea is that life forces such as those of the deer, buffalo, eagle, hawk, and bear are noble totem spirits, energies to have as one's assistants; but we must remember that *all* of life is noble. All of life gifts us with unique influences of energy which are species-specific in nature. From the breath of the tiny ant to the thundering, bellowing breath of the great elephant, each precious presence upon this earth radiates an energy frequency which in turn radiates a touchable vibration, a perceivable sound, upon the Great Web of Life. This vibration is felt by every other living being, including humans. Therefore is all of life a true totem—one to another.

PEOPLE OF THE EARTH

Aardvark
Symbology: exhibits a tendency to hide from problems
Influencing energy: strengthens self-confidence

Abyssinian cat
Symbology: honesty
Influencing energy: enhances sense of individuality and expression of same

Afghan hound
Symbology: interfering friend or associate
Influencing energy: heightens awareness of others

Agouti
Symbology: introverted personality
Influencing energy: helps one to open up more with others

Airedale terrier
Symbology: frivolous nature
Influencing energy: heightens seriousness; focus on reality

Alaskan malamute
Symbology: guidance
Influencing energy: helps to solidify one's direction in life

Alligator
Symbology: spiritual aspects which are self-serving
Influencing energy: helps to identify false logic of one's thinking

Anaconda
Symbology: restrictive personality; uptight
Influencing energy: broadens perspective; relaxes self-discipline

Ant
Symbology: cooperation
Influencing energy: instills desire to assist others; increases recognition of opportunities to volunteer

Anteater
Symbology: mental efficiency
Influencing energy: increases attention given to detail

Antelope
Symbology: free-spirited personality
Influencing energy: maintains optimism

Ape
Symbology: cautions against loss of individuality
Influencing energy: increases self-awareness of one's uniqueness

Appaloosa
Symbology: inner strength
Influencing energy: raises endurance, fortitude

Arabian horse
Symbology: noble character
Influencing energy: sheds emphasis on gentleness

Armadillo
Symbology: personal defense mechanisms
Influencing energy: increases sense of self-confidence

Asp snake
Symbology: threatening relationship
Influencing energy: exposes harmful situations and/or relationships

Aye-Aye
Symbology: acute perception
Influencing energy: heightens mental acuity

Badger
Symbology: interfering personality
Influencing energy: lessens urge to meddle in others' lives

Bandicoot
Symbology: small blessings
Influencing energy: deepens gratitude

Basenji
Symbology: sensitive nature
Influencing energy: strengthens emotional sensitivity

Basset hound
Symbology: melancholia; sadness
Influencing energy: instills emotional support

Beagle
Symbology: a sympathy-seeking friend
Influencing energy: brings insightful clarity to motives of others

Beaver
Symbology: personal and societal balance
Influencing energy: heightens ability to recognize one's spiritual aspects while balancing and utilizing life's many opportunities

Bighorn sheep
Symbology: adaptability
Influencing energy: increases awareness of one's options; deepens acceptance

Bison/buffalo
Symbology: gullibility; perseverance
Influencing energy: sharpens observational skills; raises awareness

Black bear
Symbology: overbearing personality
Influencing energy: eases tendency to manipulate others

Black widow
Symbology: dangerous individual or situation in one's life
Influencing energy: sharpens perception, intuition

Bloodhound
Symbology: intuitiveness
Influencing energy: hones perceptual skills

Boa constrictor
Symbology: smothering or constricting relationship or situation
Influencing energy: increases wariness; discernment

Boar
Symbology: haughty personality
Influencing energy: reduces egotistical attitudes

Bobcat
Symbology: withheld opinions; secretive
Influencing energy: maintains perspective on silence—the importance of keeping one's opinion to one's self

Boston terrier
Symbology: aggressive protection; distrust
Influencing energy: extends trust in others

Borzoi
Symbology: acute perception
Influencing energy: aids in recognizing dishonesty

Boxer
Symbology: protectiveness
Influencing energy: intensifies one's inner defenses

Box turtle
Symbology: endurance
Influencing energy: supplements fortitude

Brittany spaniel
Symbology: compassion
Influencing energy: heightens sense of comfort and support

Bulldog
Symbology: a bullish friend
Influencing energy: strengthens character; lessens manipulative incidences

Burmese cat
Symbology: expressive individuality
Influencing energy: deepens appreciation of one's uniqueness

Burro/donkey
Symbology: independence
Influencing energy: fortifies trust in self

Bush baby
Symbology: awareness
Influencing energy: magnifies discernment

Bushmaster snake
Symbology: dangerously manipulative personality
Influencing energy: helps to highlight harmful elements in one's life

Calf
Symbology: characterizes the beginning of an end, fatalistic element
Influencing energy: enhances perception

Calico cat
Symbology: honest friendship
Influencing energy: maintains open relationships

Camel
Symbology: tenacity; perseverance
Influencing energy: fortifies resolve and determination

Caribou/reindeer
Symbology: easily manipulated
Influencing energy: fosters independence

Centipede
Symbology: life's small irritations
Influencing energy: enhances acceptance and patience; increases understanding

Chameleon
Symbology: indecision; vacillation
Influencing energy: stabilizes self-image and bolsters strength of identity

Chamois
Symbology: gentleness
Influencing energy: softens sharp edges to personality

Cheetah
Symbology: quick wit
Influencing energy: enhances analytical thought patterns

Chihuahua
Symbology: subtle strength
Influencing energy: reinforces one's sense of self and power within

Chimpanzee/monkey
Symbology: immaturity; lacking individuality
Influencing energy: stimulates a recognition of one's inappropriate thought patterns and behavior, fosters growth

Chinchilla
Symbology: egotism; apathy
Influencing energy: widens one's awareness of others

Chipmunk
Symbology: hoarding; emotional reservation
Influencing energy: opens one up to trust and the expression of self

Chow
Symbology: inner strength
Influencing energy: heightens self-confidence

Civet
Symbology: quick wit
Influencing energy: sharpens deductive skills and responses

Coati
Symbology: industrious nature; self-reliant
Influencing energy: improves adaptability

Cobra
Symbology: threatening life aspect
Influencing energy: promotes awareness of situational elements

Cocker spaniel
Symbology: companionship; gentle associations
Influencing energy: increases depth of relationships and appreciation of same

Collie
Symbology: faithfulness
Influencing energy: intensifies sense of loyalty

Colobus monkey
Symbology: beauty of individuality
Influencing energy: deepens self-confidence

Coonhound
Symbology: retaliation
Influencing energy: eases desire for vengeance

Copperhead snake
Symbology: unexpected source of retaliation
Influencing energy: sharpens awareness, intuition

Coral snake
Symbology: subtle vindictiveness
Influencing energy: heightens discernment, wariness

Coral king snake
Symbology: misinterpretations
Influencing energy: helps to bring clarity of thought

Corn snake
Symbology: misplaced fears
Influencing energy: eases false fears; balances aspects of reality

Cottonmouth snake
Symbology: danger
Influencing energy: intensifies intuitive sense of danger or harm

Cougar/puma
Symbology: strength of quiet wisdom; patience
Influencing energy: instills greater levels of patience and perseverance

Cow
Symbology: compassion
Influencing energy: heightens sensitivity to others

Coyote
Symbology: preference for solitude
Influencing energy: balances the internal self with the external world

Crocodile
Symbology: underlying negative spiritual aspects in one's life
Influencing energy: exposes life negatives which can be corrected by the individual

Dachshund
Symbology: materialism
Influencing energy: shifts priorities away from material possessions

Daddy longlegs
Symbology: fears which are overcome
Influencing energy: instills courage

Dalmatian
Symbology: life companionship
Influencing energy: deepens quality of friendships

Dingo
Symbology: unpredictability associated with a friend
Influencing energy: sharpens acuity associated with the motives of others

Doberman Pinscher
Symbology: a law-abiding factor in one's life, usually a friend
Influencing energy: strengthens conscience

Donkey
Symbology: independence
Influencing energy: increases sense of self-reliance

Duckbill/platypus
Symbology: spiritual elements incorporated into daily living
Influencing energy: helps to assimilate spiritual philosophies into behavioral patterns

Eastern ribbon snake
Symbology: cleverness
Influencing energy: aids ingeniousness, analytical thought

Eland
Symbology: innocence and gentleness associated with strength
Influencing energy: empowers strength through gentle ness

Elephant
Symbology: a generous and gregarious nature
Influencing energy: diminishes shyness and sense of in feriority

Elk
Symbology: integrity
Influencing energy: maintains uniqueness of individuality

English foxhound
Symbology: fortitude
Influencing energy: strengthens perseverance

English setter
Symbology: loyalty
Influencing energy: strengthens relationship bonds

English sheepdog
Symbology: devotion; protective nature
Influencing energy: deepens faithfulness; intensifies support of another

Ermine
Symbology: cautions against altering self for others
Influencing energy: strengthens individuality

Fawn

Symbology: innocence; emotionally sensitive nature
Influencing energy: maintains purity of motives

Ferret

Symbology: attitudes or responses tempered with sense of humor
Influencing energy: fortifies a positive perspective and attitude

Fisher

Symbology: honesty
Influencing energy: breaks down excessive defense mechanisms

Foal

Symbology: new beginnings
Influencing energy: instills optimism

Fox

Symbology: cunning; shrewdness
Influencing energy: sharpens analytical skills

Fox terrier

Symbology: impatience
Influencing energy: raises level of patience and acceptance

Frog/toad

Symbology: impaired mental or physical condition
Influencing energy: increases self-awareness with respect to reality of self

Garter snake

Symbology: harmless qualities or aspects many fear
Influencing energy: clarifies misunderstandings

Gazelle

Symbology: naivete; innocent characteristic
Influencing energy: exposes the reality of power through simplicity

Gecko lizard
Symbology: lack of scruples
Influencing energy: initiates a questioning of motives of self

Gerbil
Symbology: a life aspect serving as a small comfort
Influencing energy: increases sense of appreciation

German shepherd
Symbology: helpful friend or associate
Influencing energy: a recognition of another's true value

Gibbon
Symbology: expressiveness
Influencing energy: maintains responsiveness; raises self-confidence

Gila monster
Symbology: cherished spiritual ideals
Influencing energy: comfort from beliefs

Giraffe
Symbology: meddling character
Influencing energy: reduces misplaced interest in the affairs of others

Gnu
Symbology: free-spirited personality
Influencing energy: maintains optimism

Goat
Symbology: gluttony of information or self-consumption
Influencing energy: slows impetuosity; introduces more logic into thought patterns

Golden retriever
Symbology: companionship
Influencing energy: amplifies sense of support

Goose
Symbology: need for more seriousness in life
Influencing energy: brings reality into sharper focus

Gopher
Symbology: multiple starts; digging around
Influencing energy: narrows options according to logic

Greyhound
Symbology: efficiency
Influencing energy: improves sense of priorities

Great Dane
Symbology: noble friend
Influencing energy: promotes greater sense of companionship

Great Pyrenees
Symbology: courage
Influencing energy: fortifies self-confidence

Greyhound
Symbology: "fast" friend or associate
Influencing energy: heightens recognition of another's habit of shallow thought

Grizzly bear
Symbology: self-absorbed personality
Influencing energy: aids in perceiving self with clarity

Groundhog/woodchuck
Symbology: fear of responsibility; hiding from reality or problems
Influencing energy: strengthens self-confidence

Guinea pig
Symbology: lack of self-confidence; fear of experience
Influencing energy: reduces anxiety

Hamster
Symbology: a life aspect serving as a small comfort
Influencing energy: increases sense of appreciation

Hedgehog/porcupine
Symbology: manipulation; subconscious defense mechanisms; tendency to "bristle and hide" from reality
Influencing energy: promotes inner strength and courage

Hippopotamus
Symbology: spiritual generosity; selflessness
Influencing energy: increases recognition of opportunities to help others

Hog/pig
Symbology: tendency to take on too much at once
Influencing energy: eases sense of over-responsibility

Honey possum
Symbology: cleverness
Influencing energy: deepens thought; increases analytical skills

Howler monkey
Symbology: egotism
Influencing energy: balances sense of self

Husky
Symbology: inner strength
Influencing energy: improves determination

Hyena
Symbology: lack of seriousness; vicious nature
Influencing energy: balances perspective and personality

Ibex
Symbology: independence
Influencing energy: enhances self-reliance

Iguana
Symbology: lack of scruples
Influencing energy: instills moral sense

Impala
Symbology: free-spirited personality
Influencing energy: maintains optimism

Irish setter
Symbology: guidance
Influencing energy: helps to clarify life choices

Irish wolfhound
Symbology: strength of character
Influencing energy: amplifies integrity

Jackal
Symbology: predatory nature
Influencing energy: gives cause for inner reflection on motives

Jackrabbit
Symbology: ingenuity
Influencing energy: aids in clarifying one's life options

Jaguar
Symbology: changeability; an altering personality
Influencing energy: balances psychological aspects

Jumping mouse
Symbology: efficiency; cleverness
Influencing energy: increases mental agility

Kangaroo
Symbology: over-protectiveness
Influencing energy: eases one into greater acceptance

Kangaroo rat
Symbology: long endurance
Influencing energy: strengthens perseverance

Keeshond
Symbology: protection
Influencing energy: sharpens intuitive awareness

Koala
Symbology: strong support
Influencing energy: instills confidence

Komondor dog
Symbology: inner strength
Influencing energy: fortifies self-reliance

Leatherback turtle
Symbology: eternal spiritual truths
Influencing energy: highlights the immutable spiritual truths, brings recognition of same

Lemming
Symbology: a follower; lack of individuality and thought
Influencing energy: increases independence

Lemur
Symbology: enigmatic aspects; obscure concepts
Influencing energy: clarifies complexities; sharpens mental focus

Leopard
Symbology: resistant to change
Influencing energy: augments manifestation of new experiences

Lhasa apso
Symbology: supportive force
Influencing energy: raises sense of encouragement

Lion
Symbology: braggart; may indicate strength of character
Influencing energy: instills recognition of inner strengths

Lizard
Symbology: lack of scruples
Influencing energy: magnifies true reflection of self

Llama
Symbology: a helper, supporter
Influencing energy: offers sense of encouragement

Loggerhead turtle
Symbology: spiritual narrow-mindedness
Influencing energy: broadens conceptual perception

Lynx
Symbology: acute observational skill; cleverness
Influencing energy: heightens one's awareness

Maltese
Symbology: close companionship
Influencing energy: deepens appreciation of special friends

Mamba
Symbology: swift retaliation
Influencing energy: lessens desire for revenge

Manchester
Symbology: loyalty
Influencing energy: raises sense of companionship

Mandrill
Symbology: perceptual amusement
Influencing energy: increases optimism

Manx cat
Symbology: unpretentiousness
Influencing energy: enhances tendency for forthrightness

Marmot
Symbology: insecurities
Influencing energy: heightens self-reliance and self-confidence

Marten
Symbology: inquisitiveness
Influencing energy: deepens curiosity; inspires wider research

Mastiff
Symbology: gentleness through inner strength
Influencing energy: maintains strong individuality

Meerkat
Symbology: community-minded; commitment; cooperation
Influencing energy: intensifies the priority of service to others

Milk snake
Symbology: character facades
Influencing energy: aids in uncovering the masks people wear

Mink
Symbology: cleverness
Influencing energy: sharpens mental acuity and analytical skills

Mole

Symbology: lack of communication; fear of reality and facing same

Influencing energy: helps to raise level of self-confidence

Mongoose

Symbology: quick wit and awareness in perceiving deception

Influencing energy: quickens responses; heightens intuition

Moose

Symbology: a spiritual burden

Influencing energy: clarifies spiritual choices

Morgan horse

Symbology: dependability

Influencing energy: deepens trust in others

Mountain goat

Symbology: determined effort to persevere

Influencing energy: energizes fortitude

Mouse

Symbology: negative aspect in one's life

Influencing energy: raises awareness of facets one needs to change in one's life

Mud turtle

Symbology: self-generated confusion

Influencing energy: brings mental clarity

Mule

Symbology: independence

Influencing energy: a realization of one's personal uniqueness and potential

Mule deer

Symbology: acute awareness

Influencing energy: intensifies observational skills

Muskrat

Symbology: repulsive attitude; revulsion

Influencing energy: increases understanding and acceptance

Norwegian elkhound
Symbology: loyalty
Influencing energy: enhances bond of friendship

Ocelot
Symbology: patience
Influencing energy: tempers impatience; expands sense of acceptance

Opossum
Symbology: backward or inverted views
Influencing energy: widens perspective to include all angles

Orangutan
Symbology: peer pressure; poor self-image
Influencing energy: strengthens individuality

Otter
Symbology: inner joy generated from spirituality
Influencing energy: instills appreciation of life's blessings

Oxen
Symbology: overwork
Influencing energy: helps to balance life patterns

Painted turtle
Symbology: small joys
Influencing energy: aids in recognition of life's little blessings

Palomino
Symbology: gentle freedom
Influencing energy: brings a quiet appreciation for one's individuality

Panda
Symbology: friend with ulterior motives
Influencing energy: heightens perspective toward others' motives

Panther
Symbology: cautious nature
Influencing energy: raises intuitive and discernment skills

Pekingese
Symbology: self-absorbed friend or associate
Influencing energy: amplifies tolerance of others

Penguin
Symbology: a successful effort
Influencing energy: fortifies determination

Percheron
Symbology: great personal efforts applied to one's path
Influencing energy: provides sense of support

Pika
Symbology: quick thinking; mental maneuverability
Influencing energy: heightens mental acuity

Polar bear
Symbology: hidden aspects of self
Influencing energy: clarifies subconscious motives

Pomeranian
Symbology: companionable affection
Influencing energy: raises sense of emotional warmth and responsiveness

Poodle
Symbology: dependability
Influencing energy: heightens sense of personal responsibility

Prairie dog
Symbology: awareness and attention given to friends within one's circle
Influencing energy: deepens feelings of camaraderie and familial responsibility

Pug
Symbology: disagreeing friend; rarely shares an opinion
Influencing energy: increases acceptance of others

Proboscis monkey
Symbology: self-assuredness
Influencing energy: intensifies self-confidence

Python
Symbology: suffocating personality, relationship, or situation
Influencing energy: highlights manipulative aspects in one's life

Quarter horse
Symbology: manipulative/domineering personality
Influencing energy: supports personal perspectives and sense of independence

Racoon
Symbology: industrious personality
Influencing energy: enriches sense of purpose

Ram
Symbology: argumentative nature; forcing desired results
Influencing energy: strengthens acceptance; increases level of patience

Rat
Symbology: a diseased element in one's life
Influencing energy: exposes negative aspects which are capable of being altered or deleted from one's life

Rattlesnake
Symbology: warning; sign of caution
Influencing energy: bolsters one's intuitive abilities

Recluse spider
Symbology: hidden dangers
Influencing energy: increases recognition of dangerous situations/relationships

Reindeer
Symbology: easily manipulated
Influencing energy: sharpens awareness of people's motives; augments personal independence

Retriever
Symbology: life helper
Influencing energy: helps to expose your true motivations

Rhesus monkey
Symbology: innocence
Influencing energy: deepens appreciation of simplicity

Rhinoceros
Symbology: controlled emotions
Influencing energy: opens up expressiveness

Rottweiler
Symbology: social selectiveness
Influencing energy: widens range of social acceptance; open to more people

Saint Bernard
Symbology: helpful or lifesaving friend
Influencing energy: clarifies perception of relationships or situations

Samoyed
Symbology: gregariousness
Influencing energy: encourages outgoing expression

Schnauzer
Symbology: a protective friend
Influencing energy: increases appreciation of those close to you

Scorpion
Symbology: retaliation
Influencing energy: encourages greater acceptance

Scottish terrier
Symbology: loyal friendship
Influencing energy: deepens allegiance and devotion

Shih Tzu
Symbology: a noble friend
Influencing energy: intensifies appreciation of loyal friends

Sheep
Symbology: lack of individuality or thought
Influencing energy: fortifies and strengthens self-confidence

Shetland pony
Symbology: concealed personal power
Influencing energy: maintains a balanced perspective toward one's abilities

Shetland sheep dog
Symbology: protective friend; watchfulness
Influencing energy: deepens appreciation of others

Shrew
Symbology: a complainer; one who is never satisfied
Influencing energy: advocates acceptance for that which is in opposition to personal views

Skye Terrier
Symbology: faithfulness
Influencing energy: deepens sense of emotional support

Siamese cat
Symbology: perceptual acuity
Influencing energy: heightens awareness

Skunk
Symbology: defense mechanisms
Influencing energy: heightens effectiveness of self-preservation methods

Sloth
Symbology: procrastination
Influencing energy: energizes self-motivational forces

Slug
Symbology: over-cautiousness
Influencing energy: lessens fear-based perceptions

Snail
Symbology: cautious awareness
Influencing energy: increases observational skills

Snapping turtle
Symbology: retaliation
Influencing energy: lessens desire for vengeance

Snow monkey
Symbology: strong sense of self
Influencing energy: strengthens individuality

Snowshoe hare
Symbology: adaptability; resourcefulness
Influencing energy: heightens perception of options

Spider
Symbology: protective measures
Influencing energy: widens perspective; sharpens intuitive skills

Spider monkey
Symbology: mental acuity
Influencing energy: intensifies analytical thought patterns

Squirrel
Symbology: hoarding
Influencing energy: raises awareness of needs rather than desires

Sugar glider
Symbology: resourcefulness
Influencing energy: clarifies potentialities and options

Tabby cat
Symbology: gregarious personality
Influencing energy: maintains companionable nature

Tapir
Symbology: a personality fault one should overcome
Influencing energy: helps to recognize personal character flaws

Tarantula
Symbology: fear-based perceptions
Influencing energy: lessens fear of reality or false fears

Tarsier
Symbology: acute perception
Influencing energy: heightens mental acuity

Tasmanian Devil
Symbology: aggressiveness
Influencing energy: lessens severity and incidence of expressed anger

Tasmanian tiger
Symbology: uncontrolled emotions; outbursts
Influencing energy: assists in maintaining self-control

Tiger
Symbology: aggressive nature; emotionally volatile
Influencing energy: balances emotions; calms impetuosity

Turtle
Symbology: fear of responsibility or reality
Influencing energy: stabilizes perspective of life

Viper
Symbology: vindictiveness
Influencing energy: balances negative and vengeful attitudes

Wallaby
Symbology: protectiveness
Influencing energy: intensifies loyalty to others

Wapiti
Symbology: integrity
Influencing energy: maintains individuality and honesty

Weasel
Symbology: evasiveness
Influencing energy: fortifies courage

Weevil
Symbology: negative traits capable of destroying one's inherent talents
Influencing energy: lessens self-destructive habits

Weimaraner
Symbology: loyalty
Influencing energy: increases sense of support

Whippet

Symbology: impetuosity

Influencing energy: slows knee-jerk reactions; heightens caution

White-tailed deer

Symbology: wariness

Influencing energy: intensifies attention given to discretion

Wildebeest

Symbology: lack of individuality

Influencing energy: lessens fear to express self

Wolf

Symbology: cleverness

Influencing energy: intensifies mental acuity; deepens wisdom

Wolverine

Symbology: vicious aggressiveness

Influencing energy: eases anger; lessens incidents of knee-jerk reactions

Wombat

Symbology: learning through example; familial associations

Influencing energy: tends to increase recall of incidents of parental lessons

Wood rat

Symbology: difficulty recognizing priorities

Influencing energy: aids in sorting out the "clutter" in one's life

Worm

Symbology: interference

Influencing energy: strengthens tolerance

Yak

Symbology: lacking discernment regarding utilization of inner strength

Influencing energy: helps clarify life options and ways to manifest skills

Yorkshire terrier
Symbology: protectiveness
Influencing energy: assists in eliminating negative aspects in one's life

Zebra
Symbology: duality of life; polarity
Influencing energy: contributes to the attainment of a more balanced life perspective

QUESTIONS ABOUT THE PEOPLE OF THE EARTH

Can any animal be one's totem?

Yes, but technically you don't pick and choose which one you'd like to have. An animal becomes your personal totem after *it comes to you* in a vivid dream or strong vision. The animal comes as a helper and guide. And it won't necessarily be one of the commonly perceived, traditional types of totems such as an eagle, bear, or owl. It could be a turtle, a snake, or a spider. Any animal can come to you in a dream or vision. Some folks believe that a specific animal totem is associated with one's birth date and is connected to your astrological birth sign, such as the deer being the totem of Sagittarius, but that's only a *surface*, generalized relationship. A true animal totem is a highly personal relationship. What I'm attempting to explain can be compared to the old American Indian tradition of naming a baby. A baby has an external, public name and it also has an internal, secret name. The reality of totems is likewise represented with generalized totems and a private one unique to the experience of the individual.

Could my tabby cat have an influence on me from its energies?

Sure it can. Every living being radiates unique energy associated with its species characteristics of cellular composition. The energy influences emanated from a domesticated being such as a cat or dog will have a greater effect upon your own receptivity because of the addition of the psychological element which connects the two of you in a manner of emotional relatedness. The animal knows its food comes directly from your hands. Your hands caress and soothe it. In turn, it responds in kind with responsive purrs or licks. In this related manner, your energy affects the pet and its energy affects you.

If, in dream symbology, an animal represents a negative life element, wouldn't it stand to reason that it would also radiate negative energy influences in the physical?

No, that's an assumption. Let's take a look at this. For example, we'll look at the symbology of the recluse spider which represents "hidden dangers." The first question you need to ask yourself is this: is this symbology a true negative? Doesn't something representing hidden dangers sound like a *positive* element? I'm sure you want to know of any hidden dangers in your life. See? Therefore, the energy influence this example radiates is one of *exposing* and *warning* you of negative aspects present in your life. It increases your recognition of dangerous situations and/or relationships by warning you to be watchful for these. Some seemingly negative symbologies will, in actuality, turn out to be the opposite. An assumed negative symbology will actually give off a positive influence.

I can't imagine a cow being anyone's totem, but my friend claims this is his. Can you help me understand this oddity?

First I'd like to comment that I personally don't perceive this as an oddity. As I previously stated in a former response, any animal being can become one's personal totem depending on one's dream or vision. A cow is no less noble than the ideology of a bear or cougar. Have we become so egomaniacal that we need macho symbols to represent our personal totems? Heaven forbid. What greater spiritual influence could a person have than one emanating the influence of compassion as the gentle cow does? Would that society as a whole be strongly affected by an increased sensitivity to others! Your confusion with this issue of your friend's stems from a misconception of what true power is. New Age thought is bloated with rhetoric describing the "power of this" and the "power of that" but no one seems to really have a grasp of what this true power is. Everyone associates it with great strength or high ability and skill. It's not. It's wisdom. It's simplicity. It's acceptance and gentleness. True power is compassion and tolerance. So a power animal totem can be a rabbit rather than a lion. People think noble is better as a totem because it reflects back a noble characteristic on the individual, but that's not so. People need to realign their thinking about what's noble because an eagle is no more noble than a chickadee, a lion no more noble than a chipmunk.

Does a turtle represent procrastination?

I imagine you deduced that because a turtle moves so slowly, but that's an error of assumption in respect to symbology. The correct symbology for a turtle is fear of reality and/or the responsibility life presents for an individual. However, the influence a turtle's energy emanates is one which stabilizes one's perspective of life. It balances the fears with self-confidence. It bolsters a belief in one's ability to cope and be a productive and effective individual.

Why doesn't a mule symbolize stubbornness?

Because people have a tendency to equate stubbornness with personal independence. When an individual cannot be manipulated by another, that individual is perceived as being problematical, obstinate, or stubborn. See? Therefore, the mule represents the beautiful independence of individuality. Its influencing energy is a positive one also, in that it emanates an increase in realizing that everyone is unique and has specific potentiality, even yourself.

How can an animal have influential energy if the species has only rare contact with people, species such as the muskrat or wildebeest? It doesn't make sense.

If such an animal is one's true and personal totem, which came in a dream or vision, it makes perfect sense because the individual needs no *physical* proximity to the animal in order for its energy influence to be effective. Yet I find this question stemming from an egocentric attitude because it's assuming that *people* make the animal's energy effective. People do not have any "activating" effect on an animal's inherent energy. Animals do not need the presence nor influence of people to give them meaning. All by themselves, animals just *are*.

Regarding the energy of animals, isn't a dog a dog?

Nope. Nada. That'd be like saying a child is a child, or a girl is a girl. What *kind* of child or girl? What ethnicity, social experience, psychological development, astrological sign, etc., comprises her makeup? All these elements combine to create a composite energy influence on others. A dog is not a dog. A dog is unique to its breed. Each breed emanates a specific energy.

I've heard of a bear being someone's animal totem, but never heard anyone make the precise distinction of it being a black bear or a grizzly bear. How come?

Perhaps the individual is keeping the specifics unpublicized as a personal element of sacredness, like one's secret name. Let's look at this. When an animal presents itself in a dream in the form of a bear, it will be a specific type of bear, won't it? It will be a black bear, or a brown bear, or a grizzly. It might even be a polar bear, but it will have species identity. A bear is not just a generic bear, it'll be one of a particular species. To say your animal totem is a bear is a generalized statement for the public, but personally, it will also have to be a particular *kind* of bear which presented itself. Another example of this is when folks claim an eagle, owl, or hawk is their totem. Why didn't they just say "bird" instead? Well, because their are so many species of birds and a dream or vision presentation is very species-specific. Either a hawk or eagle appeared to the individual or a chickadee or robin did. The term "bird" is far too generalized. Same with "bear."

PEOPLE OF THE AIR

Albatross
Symbology: burdens, sometimes self-inflicted
Influencing energy: lessens a "martyr" attitude, eases self-centeredness

Barn owl
Symbology: intuitiveness
Influencing energy: heightens perception and instincts

Barred owl
Symbology: multifaceted aspects
Influencing energy: clarifies complexities

Bat
Symbology: full utilization of spiritual intuition
Influencing energy: increases insightfulness

Bee
Symbology: industriousness; cooperative teamwork
Influencing energy: enhances associations and relationships

Bird of paradise
Symbology: elaborate thoughts/ideologies
Influencing energy: returns one to reality; lessens extravagance

Bittern
Symbology: spiritual serenity
Influencing energy: deepens solace of spiritual belief system

Blackbird
Symbology: omen; warning
Influencing energy: heightens awareness

Bluebird
Symbology: spiritual joy and contentedness
Influencing energy: deepens convictions

Blue jay
Symbology: living one's spiritual beliefs
Influencing energy: intertwines spiritual philosophies with daily behavior

Bobolink
Symbology: joy
Influencing energy: heightens life outlook

Bobwhite
Symbology: secretiveness
Influencing energy: deepens discretion

Booby
Symbology: misconceptions
Influencing energy: strengthens logic

Bowerbird
Symbology: spiritual protectiveness
Influencing energy: deepens one's sense of faith and conviction

Burrowing owl
Symbology: ability to see through others
Influencing energy: provides an acute perception into another's psychological maneuvers

Butterfly
Symbology: renewal, rejuvenation
Influencing energy: strengthens the ability to bounce back; quickens emotional recovery time

Buzzard
Symbology: gloating nature
Influencing energy: decreases tendency to "pick over remains" of another's misfortune or problems

Canada goose
Symbology: inspiration
Influencing energy: heightens incidents of insightful wisdom

Cardinal
Symbology: a highly important life element
Influencing energy: intensifies ability to prioritize and recognize priorities

Chickadee
Symbology: acceptance
Influencing energy: raises one's level of fortitude

Chicken
Symbology: fear
Influencing energy: encourages one to face life and reality

Condor
Symbology: respect
Influencing energy: heightens consideration and acceptance of others

Cormorant
Symbology: indiscriminate acceptance of spiritual concepts
Influencing energy: aids in clarifying and sorting out spiritual truths

Cowbird
Symbology: manipulation
Influencing energy: lessens desire to take advantage of others

Crane
Symbology: inquisitiveness
Influencing energy: sparks curiosity; increases desire to expand knowledge base

Crossbill
Symbology: ingenuity
Influencing energy: fosters creativity

Crow
Symbology: clear messages; straight talk
Influencing energy: clarifies communication

Cuckoo
Symbology: manipulation
Influencing energy: lessens desire to take advantage of others

Curlew
Symbology: complex thought
Influencing energy: sharpens analytical skills

Dove
Symbology: peaceful nature or condition
Influencing energy: brings balance to relationships; instills serenity

Dragonfly
Symbology: strong spiritual force in one's life
Influencing energy: raises receptivity to spiritual aspects

Duck
Symbology: spiritual vulnerability; questionable inner strength
Influencing energy: strengthens spiritual confidence and reason; fortifies strength of will

Eagle
Symbology: the self-confidence generated from an intellectual freedom to pursue knowledge
Influencing energy: raises intellectual individuality

Egret
Symbology: a spiritual sign; a spiritually related message
Influencing energy: clarifies spiritual elements entwined in daily life

Elf owl
Symbology: cleverness
Influencing energy: fortifies inventive and analytical thought

Falcon

Symbology: personal relationship with higher spiritual forces

Influencing energy: magnifies recognition of spiritual truths

Finch

Symbology: emotional maturity

Influencing energy: refines psychological reason

Firebird

Symbology: proper utilization of emotional intensity

Influencing energy: maintains emotional balance

Firefly

Symbology: intensely emotional spiritual illumination

Influencing energy: sparks intuitive spiritual wisdom, epiphanies

Flamingo

Symbology: overly optimistic

Influencing energy: aids in keeping both feet on the ground; grounding

Fly

Symbology: life aspect capable of being harmful or interfering

Influencing energy: intensifies recognition of harmful life elements

Flycatcher

Symbology: positive element in one's life

Influencing energy: helps recognize and appreciate blessings

Frigate bird

Symbology: egotism

Influencing energy: lessens need to impress others

Fruit fly

Symbology: potentially damaging element affecting personal talents

Influencing energy: increases recognition of a threat to one's abilities

Gannet
Symbology: graceful expression
Influencing energy: enhances communication skills

Geese
Symbology: instincts; inherent characteristics
Influencing energy: elevates effectiveness of actions and responses

Great-horned owl
Symbology: wisdom
Influencing energy: sharpens insight and intuitive skills

Grebe
Symbology: spiritual goodness
Influencing energy: increases expression of spiritual behavior

Grouse
Symbology: troublesome factor in one's life
Influencing energy: raises ability for problem-solving

Grosbeak
Symbology: camaraderie
Influencing energy: broadens appreciation of friendships

Grey Jay
Symbology: gregariousness
Influencing energy: maintains outgoing personality

Gull
Symbology: spiritual ideas and thoughts
Influencing energy: increases spiritual associations between concept and behavior

Harlequin duck
Symbology: individuality
Influencing energy: encourages sense of self without affectations

Hawk
Symbology: acute perceptions
Influencing energy: supplements observational skills

Heron
Symbology: beauty of spiritual wisdom
Influencing energy: reinforces inner serenity generated from utilizing wisdom in life

Honeycreeper
Symbology: life's blessings
Influencing energy: heightens recognition and appreciation of blessings

Honeyeater
Symbology: congeniality
Influencing energy: maintains gregariousness

Hornbill
Symbology: analytical thought
Influencing energy: enhances reason and logic, deductive skills

Hornet/wasp
Symbology: stinging aspects of life
Influencing energy: deepens acceptance

Horsefly
Symbology: "biting" remarks
Influencing energy: lessens tendency to make hurtful responses or comments

Hummingbird
Symbology: indecision; mental vacillation
Influencing energy: stabilizes mental focus

Ibis
Symbology: esoteric aspects to spirituality
Influencing energy: enhances recognition of higher truths

Junco
Symbology: friendship
Influencing energy: intensifies appreciation of close relationships

Killdeer
Symbology: protectiveness
Influencing energy: supplements defensive elements in one's life

Kingbird
Symbology: aggressiveness
Influencing energy: softens character

Kingfisher
Symbology: spiritual curiosity
Influencing energy: heightens desire to expand one's spiritual knowledge

Kiwi
Symbology: protectiveness
Influencing energy: aids in raising observational and awareness skills

Ladybug
Symbology: positive aspect that negates the negative and irritating facets of one's life
Influencing energy: raises one's level of acceptance with recognition of blessings which balance out life's negative facets

Lapwing
Symbology: spiritual cautiousness
Influencing energy: increases spiritual conceptual discretion

Lark bunting
Symbology: joy
Influencing energy: heightens optimism

Locust
Symbology: warns of an aspect in life with the potential to destroy spiritual belief systems
Influencing energy: heightens awareness of harmful spiritual elements

Loon

Symbology: mental or emotional confusion; convoluted thought process

Influencing energy: strengthens reason and logic

Lorikeet

Symbology: camaraderie

Influencing energy: intensifies sense of companionship

Lovebird

Symbology: companionship

Influencing energy: deepens affection; increases appreciation of others

Luna moth

Symbology: spiritual insights

Influencing energy: expands depth of spiritual understanding

Lyrebird

Symbology: inner harmony

Influencing energy: deepens sense of serenity

Magpie

Symbology: absorption of insignificant or useless concepts

Influencing energy: heightens recognition of insignificance

Meadowlark

Symbology: inner joy

Influencing energy: deepens appreciation of blessings

Mockingbird

Symbology: lack of individuality

Influencing energy: expands self-expression

Mosquito

Symbology: setback; small irritation

Influencing energy: raises acceptance level; increases patience

Moth
Symbology: destructive spiritual concepts
Influencing energy: brings spiritual discernment

Myna
Symbology: congeniality
Influencing energy: expands camaraderie

Nighthawk
Symbology: extreme high awareness
Influencing energy: heightens observation and analytical skills

Nightingale
Symbology: one's own outward expression of joy
Influencing energy: increases effect of personal optimism on others

Nutcracker
Symbology: problem solving element
Influencing energy: empowers analytical skills; endows one to perceive the less obvious options in life

Nuthatch
Symbology: ability to discover solutions
Influencing energy: brings ability to see all angles to a situation

Oriole
Symbology: helpful aspect with potential to generate negative effect if incorrectly used
Influencing energy: heightens perception of duality

Ostrich
Symbology: subconscious denials; refusal to face reality or responsibilities
Influencing energy: aids in strengthening fortitude; lessens denial tendency

Owl
Symbology: acute observations; developed awareness coupled with perceptive abilities; wisdom resulting from high spiritual enlightenment

Influencing energy: greater incidence of expressed wisdom; increased insight

Oystercatcher
Symbology: spiritual acuity
Influencing energy: sharpens spiritual intuition

Parakeet
Symbology: lack of analytical spiritual thought
Influencing energy: bestows greater measure of spiritual reason

Parrot
Symbology: verbosity
Influencing energy: lessens tendency to say a lot without saying anything

Partridge
Symbology: fearful thoughts; anxiety; paranoia; lacking self-reliance
Influencing energy: raises level of self-confidence

Peacock
Symbology: arrogance; ego
Influencing energy: clarifies true view of self

Peahen
Symbology: individuality
Influencing energy: instills confidence in one's personal uniqueness

Pelican
Symbology: spiritual gluttony; possessiveness
Influencing energy: highlights spiritual value; focuses on priority truths

Petrel
Symbology: simplicity
Influencing energy: maintains true character without affectations

Pheasant
Symbology: spiritual search

Influencing energy: centers mental focus on spiritual discovery

Phoebe

Symbology: companionship

Influencing energy: enhances relationships; intensifies bond of friendship

Pigeon

Symbology: gullibility

Influencing energy: strengthens logic and reason

Pine siskin

Symbology: fortitude

Influencing energy: heightens sense of self-reliance and endurance

Plover

Symbology: discernment

Influencing energy: sharpens observational skills

Ptarmigan

Symbology: adaptability

Influencing energy: widens scope of one's potential and resources

Puffin

Symbology: spiritual arrogance

Influencing energy: manifests a recognition of true spiritual behavior as contrasted to one's own current experience

Quail

Symbology: emotional protectiveness

Influencing energy: strengthens one's psychological defenses in a positive manner

Rail

Symbology: remembrance

Influencing energy: increases recall

Raven

Symbology: watchfulness for spiritual falsehoods and recognition of same

Influencing energy: greatly enhances spiritual awareness

Redbird

Symbology: awareness

Influencing energy: heightens observational skills

Roadrunner

Symbology: impetuosity

Influencing energy: brings greater thought applied before actions are taken

Robin

Symbology: rebirth; new beginnings or brighter perspectives

Influencing energy: brightens outlook; increases optimism

Rooster

Symbology: an awakening

Influencing energy: gives more depth to perception

Sand martin

Symbology: congeniality

Influencing energy: maintains gregariousness

Sandpiper

Symbology: spiritual slant to life

Influencing energy: aids in incorporating spiritual facets to life elements

Sapsucker woodpecker

Symbology: an effort made to rid self of negative influences

Influencing energy: encourages one to actively recognize and alter life to a more positive state

Saw-whet owl

Symbology: original thought; inventiveness

Influencing energy: increases inspiration

Screech owl

Symbology: warning

Influencing energy: raises intuitive sense

Seagull
Symbology: spiritual thoughts/perspectives
Influencing energy: enhances spiritual facets of one's daily life

Shearwater
Symbology: spiritual contentedness
Influencing energy: enhances one's faith in beliefs

Shoebill
Symbology: self-confidence
Influencing energy: enhances sense of independence

Shrike
Symbology: predatory nature
Influencing energy: lessens vindictiveness

Skylark
Symbology: happiness; joy
Influencing energy: maintains optimistic perspective

Snowbird
Symbology: encouragement
Influencing energy: instills sense of support

Snowy owl
Symbology: hidden knowledge
Influencing energy: deepens wisdom; expands intellectual horizons

Sparrow
Symbology: gentle intellectual
Influencing energy: enriches intellectual maturity

Spoonbill
Symbology: opportunistic
Influencing energy: maintains awareness of options and opportunities

Spotted owl
Symbology: inspiration
Influencing energy: increases incidents of insightful thought

Starling
Symbology: innocence
Influencing energy: enhances inner serenity in one's individuality

Stork
Symbology: new ideas or perception; new direction
Influencing energy: opens options never before considered

Sunbird
Symbology: priorities
Influencing energy: highlights important facets in one's life

Swallow
Symbology: timidness; shyness
Influencing energy: raises level of self-assuredness

Swan
Symbology: beautiful and grace-filled spiritual nature
Influencing energy: spiritual serenity

Swift
Symbology: efficiency
Influencing energy: brings recognition of inconsequential elements in one's life

Tanager
Symbology: cheerfulness; optimism
Influencing energy: raises one's perspective on life

Tern
Symbology: analytical thought
Influencing energy: increases applied reason and logic

Thrasher
Symbology: communication skills
Influencing energy: sharpens range of language, means of communicating

Thrush
Symbology: spiritual joy
Influencing energy: maintains optimism and cheerfulness

Titmouse
Symbology: ingeniousness
Influencing energy: raises analytical skills; increases perception of opportunities

Toucan
Symbology: beautiful, spiritual thoughts
Influencing energy: spiritual inspiration

Towhee
Symbology: common sense
Influencing energy: raises incidence of reasoning things out

Turkey
Symbology: hidden intelligence
Influencing energy: exposes misconceptions

Vireo
Symbology: acceptance; patience
Influencing energy: decreases emotional stress

Vulture
Symbology: aggressiveness; greed; a "user" characteristic
Influencing energy: lessens tendency to manipulate others

Warbler
Symbology: communication simplicity
Influencing energy: helps one to convey thoughts with clarity and without complexity

Waxwing
Symbology: gentle wisdom; subtle intelligence
Influencing energy: heightens effect of one's quiet wisdom on others

Weaver
Symbology: complexities
Influencing energy: sharpens analytical skills; simplifies complex concepts

Whip-Poor-Will
Symbology: melancholia
Influencing energy: raises psychological attitudes

Wood duck
Symbology: spiritual serenity
Influencing energy: deepens sense of spiritual peace

Wren
Symbology: congeniality; hospitality
Influencing energy: expands consideration of others

QUESTIONS ABOUT PEOPLE OF THE AIR

It seems to me that a raven, a blackbird, and a crow could all be grouped together to symbolize the same thing—negativity.

You most likely assume this because all of these birds are jet black, but that would be a wrong conclusion because they're each a different species with varying energy influences. The blackbird symbolizes a warning and its influence increases one's awareness and perception of such impending life elements. The crow symbolizes clear and forthright communications and brings clarity to the understanding and reception of same. The raven's message is to remind us to be watchful for spiritual falsehoods and inspires us to be intellectually sensitive to know these when we come across them. The common color of different bird species doesn't unite them into a unified grouping. As long as they're different species, they emanate different influencing energies.

Does a cuckoo bird represent stupidity?

That's a little cuckoo. Society's adaptation of nature into its slang is oftentimes way off base in its assumptions. No, the cuckoo bird does not represent stupidity or nonsense; it symbolizes manipulation and its energy influences us to guard ourselves against falling into manipulation from others and catches us whenever we are about to exhibit controlling behavior.

An eagle is my totem. Does this mean I'm special?

Your question shows that you're under the misconception that the eagle itself is more special than other species of birds or animals and, when considering the whole scope of nature, that just is not so. This is one of the common misconceptions about the ideology of totems which the general public has latched onto. People tend to think that the more majestic their totem animal appears to be, the more "special" they are to have such a noble and mighty helper. But the problem with this concept stems from not understanding that *all* of Grandmother's nature children are noble and majestic. The ego within people makes them want to be directly associated with that which they perceive as being "great" or "powerful." That's not reality. No particular animal totem is "special," therefore, no person is special due to his/her related totem. Or we could also say that every animal totem is special, therefore, everyone is special.

I have such a fascination and attraction to ladybugs, I'm wondering if they could be my totem?

Most often a totem presents itself to an individual through vivid, recurring dreams or through a strong vision; however, a powerful inherent attraction to a certain nature creature can certainly be interpreted to represent the same message—a totem for that individual. If you have such a strong attraction and feel a sense of affinity with the ladybug, then I wouldn't hesitate to say that's probably your personal totem. I think it's a wonderful totem to have because the ladybug symbolizes a positive aspect which negates the negative and irritating facets of one's life. The ladybug raises one's level of acceptance through recognition of the little blessings which serve to balance out life's negative aspects. This is a powerful gift. This is a great spiritual attribute to have. To be able to accept life and cherish the small blessings that come one's way is truly a divine characteristic. I like ladybugs, too.

What is Summer Rain's animal totem?

Everywhere I've lived, great-horned owls have presented themselves to me. They've come singly and in multiple sets of pairs. They've chortled above me on tree branches and hooted from the perch of my split-rail fencing twenty feet from my back door. They've glided ten feet above my head and sat atop my cabin roof. Symbols and physical signs of the great-horned owl have come into my life quite unexpectedly over the years. I don't personally claim to have a particular totem, yet the great-horned owl appears to have adopted me and I joyfully accept its friendship and reach out to hold its wing in companionship during my walk through this life.

Pheasants have begun to hang around my wooded property. Is this some kind of nature sign?

It's possible that the pheasant is attracted to you for the purpose of being a personal totem; however, you also said in your letter that this appears to occur during hunting season and your property is off limits to hunters. Birds and wild animals are extremely wise to the shifting seasons and the safer regions to retreat to during the hunting time of humans. I tend to think that these pheasants are seeking safety on your land as a sanctuary from the hunters.

Why doesn't a rooster symbolize pride?

Let's not put assumed characteristics to the nature people. Just because a rooster struts about the barnyard doesn't mean it represents pride or arrogance. First and foremost it announces the break of day, the dawning of a fresh and new experience. The rooster symbolizes "an awakening" which has the potentiality of bringing wisdom and higher insights. The rooster represents greater depth to one's perception. No, it isn't a symbol for pride.

What does a flicker represent?

A flicker is a species of woodpecker. Like the sapsucker, it symbolizes self-improvement and encourages one to perceive and change his/her life to a more positive state of beingness.

Are a wood duck and a harlequin duck the same thing?

Though they're both equally beautiful water fowl with highly distinctive characteristic markings, they are different species of ducks and, consequently, have different energy influences. The wood duck symbolizes spiritual serenity and emanates an influence which assists in conveying one's thoughts with greater clarity and simplicity. The harlequin duck, on the other hand, symbolizes individuality and its energy exudes an influence which encourages a sense of true self without any form of false affectations.

What does a camp robber bird represent?

A camp robber is another common name for a grey jay. The grey jay symbolizes a gregarious personality and influences people to maintain their cheerfulness and optimistic outlook on life.

Are there different symbologies for a white swan and a black swan? It seems to me that they'd be different.

In this instance a swan is still a swan, which symbolizes a beautiful and grace-filled spiritual nature. It's influence is to bestow and deepen one's sense of spiritual serenity. The influence of the swan does not particularly stem from its color, but more concretely from its character and manner of movement through the *water* (which symbolizes *spiritual* aspects of life). The black swan moves no differently from the white; therefore, they both represent the same message and emanate the same influencing force.

Do water fowl have different energies than land birds?

As a general rule water fowl will more often symbolize spiritual aspects because water represents the spiritual facet of life. Yet many species of land birds will also indicate a spiritual association. For instance, a bluebird symbolizes spiritual joy and contentedness, while the Canada goose symbolizes inspiration.

Do seagulls living in the mountains have a different symbology than those dwelling by the sea?

I found this to be an interesting question. I suppose those people living on the seacoasts would be mighty surprised to know that we have seagulls soaring over our mountain ridges. I even have some flying over my cabin once in awhile. The influence of seagulls comes from their unique, individual species, not from the location they choose to dwell in. Their biological makeup is what creates their specific energy influence and symbology, so their location has no effect on these. The seagull—no matter where it dwells—symbolizes spiritual thoughts and perspectives. Its influencing energy emanates an enhancement of the spiritual elements of one's daily life.

Is a wild finch's energy different than a caged, pet shop finch?

Again, like the former question and answer, the premise is the same. A bird's symbology and energy influence is generated from its cellular composition, not from where it dwells. A wild finch will symbolize and emanate influences exactly like those of a domesticated one.

PEOPLE OF THE WATERS

Abalone

Symbology: inherent beauty of spiritual gifts, talents, or knowledge

Influencing energy: brings recognition of power being spiritual behavior

Albacore tuna

Symbology: spiritual generosity

Influencing energy: increases incidences of give-aways

Algae

Symbology: spiritually nourishing life aspect

Influencing energy: brings blessings to the fore

Algae-eater

Symbology: spiritual discernment

Influencing energy: heightens recognition of spiritual opportunities and blessings

Anchovy

Symbology: spiritual aspect not readily accepted

Influencing energy: highlights the importance of all spiritual truths, especially those which are difficult for one to accept

Angelfish

Symbology: finer aspects of spiritual truths

Influencing energy: clarifies higher spiritual concepts above commonly known and accepted generalities

Anglerfish

Symbology: spiritual indecision

Influencing energy: brings clarity of spiritual concepts into focus

Archerfish

Symbology: spiritual focus

Influencing energy: sharpens and defines spiritual direction

Barb

Symbology: self-righteousness

Influencing energy: lessens need to chastise another's spiritual belief or behavior; raises level of spiritual tolerance

Barracuda

Symbology: lack of moral or ethical value; vicious personality

Influencing energy: returns increasing measures of spiritual behavior to one's life

Bass

Symbology: generosity

Influencing energy: increases incidents of sharing, volunteer work

Batfish

Symbology: inherent spiritual understanding

Influencing energy: maintains comprehension of higher truths

Blenny

Symbology: spiritual focus, centeredness

Influencing energy: heightens direction and fortitude

Blindfish

Symbology: spiritual indecision, confusion

Influencing energy: clarifies direction

Bloodsucker/leech

Symbology: manipulation; one who diminishes the motivation of another

Influencing energy: heightens recognition of a "user" personality

Blowfish

Symbology: spiritual verbosity

Influencing energy: lessens tendency to preach insignificant concepts

Bluegill
Symbology: spiritual joy
Influencing energy: heightens inner sense of spiritual warmth

Blue whale
Symbology: spiritual generosity
Influencing energy: raises recognition of opportunities to help others

Boxfish
Symbology: spiritual confinements; rigidness
Influencing energy: helps to expand one's spiritual horizons; raises tolerance

Brain coral
Symbology: spiritual knowledge and wisdom
Influencing energy: deepens wisdom and increases its behavior expression

Bullhead
Symbology: spiritual obstinance
Influencing energy: increases tolerance, acceptance

Butterfish
Symbology: spiritual vacillation
Influencing energy: helps to focus perspective on singular spiritual concepts

Butterfly fish
Symbology: spiritual joy
Influencing energy: maintains one's depth of faith

Candlefish
Symbology: spiritual solace, dependence
Influencing energy: maintains faith as an emotional foundation, touchstone

Cardinal fish
Symbology: spiritual arrogance; egotism
Influencing energy: decreases need for spiritual superiority

Carp

Symbology: spiritual nitpicking

Influencing energy: lessens tendency to criticize another's beliefs

Catfish

Symbology: "cattiness" for one's spiritual belief; pretentious and arrogant spiritual attitude

Influencing energy: lessens spiritual arrogance and self-righteousness

Catshark

Symbology: spiritual discernment; aggressive watchfulness

Influencing energy: maintains observational skills

Chubb

Symbology: spiritual gluttony; indiscriminate conceptual acceptance

Influencing energy: helps to focus on main concepts of truth

Cichlid

Symbology: spiritual companionship

Influencing energy: enhances depth of spiritual camaraderie and support

Clown fish

Symbology: foolish factors connected to one's spiritual beliefs

Influencing energy: returns clarity to spiritual beliefs; strengthens reason and logic

Cockleshell

Symbology: remains of one's feelings; residual emotions

Influencing energy: aids in releasing potentially harmful memories

Codfish

Symbology: spiritual arrogance

Influencing energy: reduces sense of spiritual superiority

Conch shell
Symbology: cherished spiritual aspects
Influencing energy: deepens appreciation of beliefs

Coral
Symbology: one's spiritual attributes/talents
Influencing energy: increases utilization of spiritual gifts

Coralfish
Symbology: spiritual protectiveness
Influencing energy: lessens tendency to guard beliefs from outside influences

Coral reef
Symbology: fragile balance of maintaining spiritual equilibrium within the physical plane of existence
Influencing energy: maintains balance of spiritual and physical aspects

Cowfish
Symbology: spiritual generosity, largess
Influencing energy: enhances potential for exercising spiritual talents

Crab
Symbology: negativity
Influencing energy: raises optimism and positive attitude

Crappie
Symbology: indecision
Influencing energy: aids in establishing a focus; helps define direction

Crayfish
Symbology: a voluntary withdrawal from an agreed-upon event or responsibility
Influencing energy: stresses personal integrity

Danio
Symbology: spiritual confusion
Influencing energy: helps to unravel spiritual complexity

Darter

Symbology: vacillation

Influencing energy: lessens need to jump from one spiritual concept to another

Dolphin

Symbology: spiritual companionship

Influencing energy: deepens appreciation of close relationships

Eel

Symbology: spiritual vacillation

Influencing energy: stabilizes fluctuations in spiritual beliefs

Filefish

Symbology: spiritual basics

Influencing energy: increases ability to simplify complex concepts

Flathead

Symbology: spiritual narrow-mindedness

Influencing energy: widens scope of tolerance and acceptance

Flounder

Symbology: spiritual faltering

Influencing energy: supports times of spiritual doubt

Flying fish

Symbology: spiritual application

Influencing energy: expands potentiality for expression of spiritual talents

Frogfish

Symbology: spiritual vacillation

Influencing energy: helps to ground beliefs

Goatfish

Symbology: spiritual independence; following personal path

Influencing energy: strengthens unique convictions

Goby

Symbology: spiritual individuality; unique beliefs

Influencing energy: supports personal spiritual direction and foundational beliefs

Goldfish

Symbology: spiritually confining situation, belief, or condition

Influencing energy: brings recognition of a spiritual stagnation

Gourami

Symbology: camaraderie

Influencing energy: intensifies sense of spiritual friendship and companionship

Grayling

Symbology: spiritual commonality; traditional dogma

Influencing energy: inspires spiritual individuality

Grouper

Symbology: lacking spiritual individuality; needing support for beliefs

Influencing energy: brings greater self-confidence and faith in one's beliefs

Grunion

Symbology: lack of spiritual independent thought

Influencing energy: inspires personal expansion

Guppy

Symbology: a spiritual neophyte

Influencing energy: heightens desire for deeper, higher spiritual knowledge

Haddock

Symbology: traditional beliefs

Influencing energy: expands one's interest to reach for higher truths

Halibut

Symbology: spiritual nourishment

Influencing energy: increases spiritual behavior

Harp seal

Symbology: innocence; spiritual vulnerability

Influencing energy: maintains spiritual purity and strengthens character

Hermit crab

Symbology: spiritual reclusiveness; solace

Influencing energy: heightens appreciation of beliefs

Herring

Symbology: spiritual bounty; blessings

Influencing energy: deepens recognition of life's positive facets

Jellyfish

Symbology: lack of firm convictions; using one's "stinging" defense mechanisms to maintain an air of "free-floating" irresponsibility

Influencing energy: increases integrity, personal responsibility

Jewelfish

Symbology: spirituality as one's most valued priority in life

Influencing energy: maintains importance of beliefs

Kelp

Symbology: spiritual health

Influencing energy: maintains one's faith in beliefs

Killer whale

Symbology: spiritual generosity, magnanimity

Influencing energy: maintains spiritual integrity and largess

Kingfish

Symbology: spiritual superiority

Influencing energy: decreases arrogance; increases tolerance for another's belief

Lantern fish

Symbology: inspiration; epiphanies

Influencing energy: increases incidents of inspiration

Leatherjacket
Symbology: spiritual insulation
Influencing energy: decreases fear of losing faith

Lionfish
Symbology: spiritual arrogance; self-righteousness
Influencing energy: reduces spiritual egotism

Loach
Symbology: spiritual procrastination; laziness
Influencing energy: revitalizes one's spiritual interest

Lungfish
Symbology: spiritual accoutrements
Influencing energy: reduces need for physical enhancements to spiritual beliefs

Lyretail
Symbology: spiritual verbosity; superfluous facets
Influencing energy: streamlines beliefs; rids self of extraneous elements

Mackerel
Symbology: unexpected event or development
Influencing energy: raises level of acceptance

Manatee
Symbology: spiritual largess; being generous with one's talents
Influencing energy: enhances potential for sharing spiritual abilities

Man-o-war
Symbology: spiritual intolerance
Influencing energy: lessens arrogance; raises acceptance

Manta ray
Symbology: attractive spiritual aspects which could prove to be dangerous
Influencing energy: heightens spiritual discernment

Marlin

Symbology: spiritual focus; centered spiritual attention

Influencing energy: maintains spiritual course; lessens distractive elements

Minnow

Symbology: spiritual insecurity

Influencing energy: reinforces confidence in beliefs

Mollie

Symbology: traditional spiritual beliefs

Influencing energy: expands one's scope of spiritual search

Moonfish

Symbology: spiritual wisdom

Influencing energy: expands living application of gained wisdom

Moor

Symbology: esoteric aspects of spiritual concepts

Influencing energy: clarifies complex ideologies; dispels mystery

Moray eel

Symbology: spiritual aggressiveness and over-exuberance

Influencing energy: serves to calm over-enthusiasm and/or forcefulness

Mullet

Symbology: superfluous spiritual element

Influencing energy: highlights spiritual priorities, the immutable truths

Mussel

Symbology: spiritual protectiveness bordering on reclusiveness

Influencing energy: aids in turning secretiveness into solace

Needlefish

Symbology: spiritual complexity

Influencing energy: raises level of understanding

Neon tetra
Symbology: a spiritual "light" to pay attention to
Influencing energy: highlights spiritual priorities regarding conceptual truths

Octopus
Symbology: spiritual flailing
Influencing energy: brings greater spiritual focus into one's life

Otter
Symbology: spiritual joy
Influencing energy: heightens recognition of inner joy stemming from spiritual beliefs

Oyster
Symbology: fear of anything new or having to interact with others
Influencing energy: expands self-confidence

Paddlefish
Symbology: self-generated spiritual journey
Influencing energy: encourages one to seek personal direction and path

Parrotfish
Symbology: spiritual verbosity; imitation
Influencing energy: limits tendency to preach

Penguin
Symbology: successful efforts
Influencing energy: deepens personal reward from efforts applied

Perch
Symbology: spiritual neutrality; lack of spiritual direction
Influencing energy: enhances spiritual interest; strengthens search

Pickerel
Symbology: spiritual greed or arrogance
Influencing energy: balances personal perspective of spiritual aspects

Pike
Symbology: spiritual nourishment, fulfillment
Influencing energy: increases depth of spiritual benefits and gifts

Pilot fish
Symbology: an imitated spiritual path
Influencing energy: inspires individuality of one's direction

Pipefish
Symbology: rigid spiritual beliefs
Influencing energy: widens one's perspective, tolerance, and acceptance

Piranha
Symbology: spiritual narrow-mindedness; vicious possessiveness of one's beliefs
Influencing energy: reduces self-righteousness

Plankton
Symbology: spiritual foundation or basics
Influencing energy: strengthens spiritual principles

Platy
Symbology: traditional spiritual beliefs
Influencing energy: broadens one's reach for spiritual expansion

Porcupine fish
Symbology: spiritual defensiveness
Influencing energy: widens perception and acceptance of varying beliefs

Porkfish
Symbology: spiritual fulfillment
Influencing energy: broadens scope of beliefs and experiential actualization

Porpoise
Symbology: spiritual companionship
Influencing energy: enhances spiritual associations

Psychedelic fish

Symbology: spiritual confusion; lack of conceptual discernment

Influencing energy: brings clarity and focus to one's search

Puffer fish

Symbology: potentially dangerous spiritual element which one should defend self against

Influencing energy: fortifies personal defenses

Rasbora

Symbology: spiritual enjoyment

Influencing energy: enhances appreciation of one's beliefs

Redfish

Symbology: important spiritual concepts

Influencing energy: encourages focus on main truths to beliefs

Red snapper

Symbology: spiritual intolerance

Influencing energy: raises level of acceptance and tolerance of another's belief

Remora

Symbology: spiritual basics

Influencing energy: reminds one of basic spiritual behavior

Sailfish

Symbology: spiritual destiny

Influencing energy: sharpens one's focus on spiritual path

Salamander

Symbology: blind to the spiritual elements of daily life

Influencing energy: raises awareness of opportunity to utilize or receive spiritual talents or blessings

Salmon

Symbology: going against a spiritual current/instinct

Influencing energy: helps one to "flow" with life; acceptance

Sand dollar
Symbology: spiritual riches
Influencing energy: increases recognition of life's little blessings which come one's way

Sawfish
Symbology: spiritual discernment
Influencing energy: strengthens ability to "cut through" superfluous spiritual aspects

Scallop
Symbology: ingestion of harmful spiritual elements
Influencing energy: aids in recognizing dangerous concepts

Scorpion fish
Symbology: deadly spiritual element
Influencing energy: sharpens intuitiveness regarding spiritual concepts

Sea anemone
Symbology: spiritual diversity
Influencing energy: enhances one's utilization of spiritual talents

Sea cucumber
Symbology: societal spiritual beliefs; traditional dogma
Influencing energy: clarifies commonly held tenets from truth

Sea fan
Symbology: spiritual vacillation
Influencing energy: stabilizes perceptual ideologies

Sea horse
Symbology: illogical spiritual search or belief which may indicate more fantasy than reality; wild spiritual concepts
Influencing energy: brings spiritual reason and logic into thought process

Seal
Symbology: living spiritual beliefs

Influencing energy: enhances spiritual behavior and serenity of same

Seashell
Symbology: spiritual gifts and talents
Influencing energy: deepens rewards of utilizing one's spiritual abilities

Sea slug
Symbology: spiritual laziness; spiritual entrapment
Influencing energy: frees one from accepting a "forced" dogma

Sea snail
Symbology: slow and methodical spiritual pace based on one's level of comprehension
Influencing energy: creates a comfortable, satisfying sense of one's current level of spiritual development, journey

Sea sponge
Symbology: spiritual over-absorption
Influencing energy: increases conceptual discrimination and integrity

Sea turtle
Symbology: cautious spiritual search or journey
Influencing energy: maintains spiritual wariness and analytical reasoning

Sea urchin
Symbology: spiritual immaturity
Influencing energy: raises level of understanding

Seaweed
Symbology: spiritual indecision; vacillation
Influencing energy: aids in creating a spiritual focus based on personal perceptions

Shad
Symbology: spiritual insignificance
Influencing energy: highlights superfluous spiritual facets

Shark

Symbology: religious fanaticism

Influencing energy: hones recognition of spiritual arrogance and self-righteousness

Shrimp

Symbology: finer spiritual truths

Influencing energy: instills deeper understanding of higher truths

Siamese fighting fish

Symbology: spiritual argumentiveness

Influencing energy: calms tendency to debate concepts and/or the spiritual beliefs of others

Smelt

Symbology: small spiritual insights

Influencing energy: increases incidents of enlightened inspiration

Soldierfish

Symbology: spiritual fanaticism

Influencing energy: lessens intolerance of another's belief system

Sole

Symbology: spiritual individuality; independent thought

Influencing energy: inspires unique conceptual truths; enhances spiritual wisdom

Squid

Symbology: haphazard spiritual search

Influencing energy: clarifies direction, purpose

Squirrelfish

Symbology: hoarding of spiritual gifts

Influencing energy: opens one's options and opportunities to share blessings

Starfish

Symbology: spiritual truths

Influencing energy: aids in highlighting truths of spiritual reality from traditional beliefs

Stickleback
Symbology: spiritual intolerance
Influencing energy: relaxes rigid thought; increases acceptance of other spiritual possibilities

Stingray
Symbology: false prophet, teacher
Influencing energy: helps to perceive self-righteous and arrogant spiritual leaders

Stonefish
Symbology: spiritual fanaticism
Influencing energy: decreases intolerance

Sturgeon
Symbology: strong spiritual faith
Influencing energy: maintains strength of convictions

Sucker fish
Symbology: spiritual gullibility
Influencing energy: strengthens spiritual discernment

Sunfish
Symbology: joy in one's spirituality
Influencing energy: raises inner fulfillment of spiritual belief and exhibited behavior

Surgeonfish
Symbology: analytical thought
Influencing energy: maintains high level of reason and logic

Swordtail
Symbology: spiritual defensiveness
Influencing energy: lessens need to defend one's spiritual beliefs

Tadpole
Symbology: spiritual immaturity; a novice
Influencing energy: stabilizes urge to seek beyond one's understanding

Tarpon
Symbology: narrow-mindedness

Influencing energy: broadens one's perspective and acceptance

Tetra

Symbology: spiritual fragility

Influencing energy: increases strength of delicate spiritual beliefs

Threadfin

Symbology: finer aspects of spiritual concepts

Influencing energy: increases discernment and analytical thought

Triggerfish

Symbology: spiritual aggressiveness

Influencing energy: decreases tendency toward intolerance, fanaticism

Tripodfish

Symbology: lack of conceptual comprehension

Influencing energy: raises level of understanding

Trout

Symbology: spiritual contentedness

Influencing energy: brings satisfaction with one's spirituality

Unicornfish

Symbology: rare spiritual comprehension

Influencing energy: maintains high level of understanding; The Knowing

Viper fish

Symbology: spiritual skepticism

Influencing energy: widens perspective and deepens reason

Walrus

Symbology: spiritual accuracy; true righteousness

Influencing energy: brings solace and comfort from beliefs

Water snake

Symbology: spiritual element which may be dangerous

Influencing energy: heightens recognition of life aspects containing duality

Whitefish

Symbology: spiritual clarity

Influencing energy: brings spiritual concepts into focus

Wrasse

Symbology: spiritual behavior, expression

Influencing energy: heightens potentiality for enacting spiritual beliefs in life

Yellow tang

Symbology: spiritual behavior

Influencing energy: creates increased manifestation of spiritual beliefs enacted and entwined in daily life

QUESTIONS ABOUT THE PEOPLE OF THE WATERS

How can fish have any kind of influence on people if the fish are in the water?

This is very much like the question regarding wild animals such as the wildebeest and muskrat, which rarely come in contact with humans. Technically, all living creatures upon this planet have energy and specific influences emanating from that unique energy. People do not activate that energy. That energy does not need people to make it effective or meaningful. The creatures inhabiting the waters of earth generate their own species-specific energy all on their own. Energy surrounded by water neither diminishes nor intensifies it. That energy just is.

How can a fish be a totem?

The same way a deer, bear, or owl can be. Remember, a totem is a sign representing a form of spirit guidance and assistance. A totem presents itself within dreamscapes and visions. It is not a *physical* encounter but rather an ethereal one. It's a symbolic representation which conveys a message for the individual. More than its physical characteristics, its energy influence is the main aspect of a totem. And that's where people get so hung up on misunderstanding the possibility of having an ant for a totem rather than a big, strong bear. There is *power* contained within every energy influence. Spiritual serenity is power. Acceptance is power. Unconditional goodness is power. Power does not equate to muscle strength or size. The totem influence of a butterfly or a sea snail is as powerful as that of an eagle or bear. All of these emanate differing influences, yet they all are equally powerful in their own right. The surround of water creates no barrier to these influences of the water people.

How can a seashell radiate active influence from its former energy if it's a vacated shell?

First of all, the energy of it is not "former" energy, it's current viable energy because that shell, though the living biological life form of it has vacated it, is still comprised of the cellular DNA which created it and made it a facet of a separate, individual species. That shell still has its original molecular composition. That composition is what the influential energy emits from.

A stonefish behaves like its namesake, a stone. How can that creature represent any type of active behavioral influence?

Influences from a creature's energy have a direct relationship to its outward behavioral expression and habits. Though the stonefish's appearance is that of a rock sitting on the sea floor, it is far from an innocent-looking stone. It's behavior is *not* as a stone when something touches it or steps on it. It immediately, instinctively retaliates without reserve or discrimination. Appearance in no way reflects behavioral characteristics and we must be careful not to assume they do.

Do we absorb totem energies when we ingest the animal? Say deer meat or trout?

Oh my gosh, I'm not at all comfortable with this question. I'm not even going to get into the issue of eating *deer*, so let's move forward to the main point of the question. Totem energy influences are not absorbed through one's stomach. These influences are radiated out into the ether where the intended recipient's own responsiveness becomes its destination. This energy is not physical, but is a type of spiritual energy which influences another. This energy has consciousness and is a vital facet of the living consciousness of the great Web of Life. To reduce this magnificent greatness to the dark putridness of one's stomach is more than ridiculous, it's sacrilegious. Totem energies emanate from one's living beingness to another's living consciousness. That is how it moves along the strong, silken threads which make up the great living Web of Life.

If seaweed radiates influential energy, can it be a totem?

This question is not as silly as it may sound. No, seaweed cannot be anyone's totem, though it still emanates energy influence. As a rule of thumb, a totem can be any living creature with a face. Plants give off energy which manifest influences, but they cannot be an individual's personal totem. The confusion comes from the fact that *all* of life radiates energy, so we tend to think all life is all-inclusive regarding the ideology of totems. Remember, simply put, only those life forms having a face can be a totem.

If a tadpole was someone's totem, how does it stay a totem when it changes into a frog?

You're assuming that this tadpole totem is a singular individual when that wouldn't be the case regarding the ideology of totems. Tadpole totem energy remains tadpole energy for the individual. This energy doesn't metamorphize into frog energy. The totem influence remains that energy type at the tadpole *stage* of its development. See what I mean? One doesn't adopt a specific, individual tadpole which soon matures into a frog bearing replacement frog energy. The totem isn't a *physical* tadpole, but the *energy influence* of the tadpole.

I have a large aquarium and am very much attracted to all types of fish having long, wavy fins and tails. Can you tell me why I have this particular draw to these?

An aquarium itself represents a desire to bring spiritual facets into the home, to have these in close proximity to your beingness. What you're drawn to put into that aquarium gives additional depth to the rationale for the tank. Having a special affinity to those fish with long, wavy tails represents an appreciation of spirituality's delicate beauty. The diaphanous fantails and multicolor aspects express this beauty and spectacular magnificence of spirituality and so exemplify your own sensitivity in recognizing these and cherishing them.

Do fish in fresh water have different energy influences than those in sea water?

No, because the influences come directly from the particular *species* of fish rather from the water which surrounds them. Likewise, seaweed from the ocean will not have a different energy influence from that of an inland lake. Biological composition, the cellular makeup is what the energy emanates from.

Does a puffer fish symbolize spiritual egotism?

That would be a logical assumption, but assumptions often don't equate to reality. A puffer fish symbolizes a dangerous spiritual aspect in one's life which the individual needs to identify and defend self against. The influence of this fish aids in fortifying one's personal spiritual defenses.

My sister says I'm silly not to eat fish, but I claim that they have social behavior and emotional expression, and shouldn't be viewed as expendable people of the planet. Comment?

Anyone spending any time at all observing the divergent life forms swimming in an aquarium eventually observes undeniable community behavior. Anyone working with or visiting a dolphin exhibit will, without a doubt, walk away with a revised philosophy about these water people's consciousness. Also, these beings have *faces*! I think your sister needs to develop her observational skills and take a closer look at her "relatedship" to all living beings who share this planet with her.

I don't think I have an animal totem. Does that mean I don't need one or that I'm not special enough for one to come to me?

Neither. Not everyone has a totem. Although I seem to attract great-horned owls, I don't perceive them as being an actual totem, *per se*. Not having a recognizable totem does not equate to not being special enough nor does it mean that you don't need one. Accept what is without drumming up inconsequential analyzations which only complicate your life with insignificant complexities. Accept reality as is. To continually question life is to impose an iron barrier to acceptance. In turn, this causes self-imposed stress and restlessness which locks serenity outside the door of your life. To question every little facet of life is to not understand the mechanics of the natural order. To have to analyze every little aspect of life and weigh it upon a direct associative scale of self is to be self-centered, wherein one is constantly relating every thing to the I. Your question was a valid one and I'm not saying that it was self-centered; yet it contains an ego-relatedness thought process that asks for verification of your status in the scheme of things. It has duality. It asks if you're so special that you don't need a totem or if you're not special enough for one to present itself to you. You're asking if you're a Somebody or a Nobody. You're neither . . . you're You! Having a totem does not imply that an individual is in any way "special." This is very important to understand. Having one is no more special than having a microwave in your kitchen when your neighbor doesn't. So what? Reality is what it is. Some folks carry a good luck charm, others don't. Some people have a favorite number, others couldn't care less about having an affinity with a particular number. It's individuality. It's nothing special—just reality

SECTION II

Grandmother's Gifts of Spirit

Gifts from Her Spirit

We don't often think of receiving gifts from Grandmother Earth's beautiful Spirit, but She is constantly showering us with sparkling insights of intuition, sudden epiphanies of wisdom, and endless, symbolic messages in our nightly dream journeys. The beingness of Her very Nature impregnates our world with Her living consciousness, Her eternal Spirit. Her nature continually instructs us. Her spirit, forever nurtures our growth into the brighter light and higher understanding of true reality. From the industriousness and cooperative efforts of the ant's nature to the acute observational awareness of the owl, She provides us with endless multitudes of examples to learn from. Totems presenting in visions and dreams can serve to support and encourage our life efforts. Dreamscapes open our consciousness to the formerly hidden keys to unlocking the awake-state daily confoundments which trouble our minds and muddy the clarity of choices and decision-making. Our paths are more defined through the messages of dreams and visions, and the wisdom

Grandmother Earth continually attempts to lay before our every footfall along our long, twisting life trails. The following represents questions about the intuition, wisdom and dream symbols that my readers have written me about over the years.

INTUITION, WISDOM, AND DREAM SYMBOLOGY

Are people born with natural intuition or is it a skill to be personally developed?

Intuition is an inherent attribute of the human consciousness. Consciousness, as referenced here, means that eternal, living essence of the human spirit which never dies and is inherently cognizant of all facets of every vibrational dimension of reality. This equates to a personal energy which is firmly connected through a thread of interrelatedness with all living things. Consciousness, even in this day and age, is a matter of puzzlement to neuroscientists, who are still attempting to come up with adequate terminology to succinctly define it.

Yet the crux of their dilemma is generated from their misconception that consciousness is bounded by a mechanized brain. They're basing their goal of defining on a false foundation which claims that consciousness is solely supported by synapses of intercellular currents of electrical impulses. But this is not the fact of the matter. This is not the supporting cornerstone of consciousness; spirit is. Since spirit is eternal and its potentiality for reaching out into the multitudinous realms of reality is limitless, consciousness has no bounds nor ties to the physical, three-dimensional plane of existence. In this manner is consciousness and its characteristic quality for intuition a natural and inherent attribute of the human being.

Everyone has intuitiveness. It's externalized and exhibited more commonly in women because the feminine energy is more attuned to the spirit and non-material aspect of reality. That's where the phrase "women's intuition" came from. Women have a stronger mental connection to the eternally active consciousness of self, where awareness and acute perceptive activity are continually taking place. Historically, this fact has been generally evidenced through their many experiential expressions of such ongoing events throughout their lives. The tendencies of society can be somewhat amusing when, for example, men will snicker about "women's intuition" and then, without hesitation, claim they were right about something because they had this strong "gut feeling." I suppose men feel more manly claiming the "gut feeling" rather than attributing their higher sense of foresight to "women's intuition."

Yet the bottom line of this concept is not relegated to any type of gender-specific phraseology by which we each individually choose to define this higher sense of our consciousness. The bottom line is the basic fact that intuition is inherent in each human being through her/his consciousness. And access is available to everyone . . . but only if you listen and then act on that which is heard. So many times people shrug off their intuitive thoughts, then later chastise themselves for not having given them credence and acting on them.

These thoughts come to us for a reason. They have purpose. They are messages of foreknowledge which come to aid our footfalls in life and assist in clarifying our directional choices and are oftentimes in the form of actual forewarnings. It's common knowledge that animals have instincts, yet few people realize that humans do, too. Intuition is what society has ultimately termed that human instinct.

What is wisdom?

Well, I could give you the Webster's New Universal Unabridged Dictionary definition which is this: "The quality or state of being wise." But this leads to asking, what does being wise mean? So the dictionary doesn't truly define wisdom, does it? Wisdom involves so much more than just simply saying it's a state of being wise. Wisdom encompasses various separate important qualities or types of perceptual and behavioral actualizations within an individual's developed nature. Wisdom is not knowledge. Wisdom is not intelligence. Wisdom is not book learning. So, what is it then? Wisdom is the power of attained spiritual maturity and the experiential manifestation of same throughout life. Okay, fine, so what's spiritual maturity? Well, to encapsulate it, it's having acceptance and tolerance of others, patience, compassion, understanding, perseverance, knowing when silence serves best, forbearance, a deep respect for all of life, and the daily practice of unconditional goodness. These are the essential cells which make up the entity of wisdom.

How does one tell the difference between a dream comprising fragmented elements of one's day and a dream containing a meaningful message?

The answer is contained within the wording of your question. If a dream is noticeably fragmented, it's usually a haphazard replay of one's day through the presentation of remnant symbology. The obvious nonsensical elements of dreams highlight the fact that they're fractured—a mosaic representation of the multiple elements of one's experiential past. When a dream is meant to be a message of some type, it will unfold with a more sequential order than a fragmented one. A message dream will convey an overall focused thought, concept, or ideology. It will usually cause deep thought and extensive reflection upon awakening, which is meant to generate analytical contemplation geared to culminate in gained insight. The insight of these dream messages are most often those life elements of which we're already subconsciously aware but, for one reason or another—usually a psychological reason—don't consciously acknowledge.

Sometimes denial is the reason. Sometimes lack of acceptance is another; other times an unwillingness to face personal responsibility is the reason we don't consciously acknowledge the facts of life. Whatever the reason, consciousness holds and retains the facts of the matter without reserve or judgement. That consciousness recognizes when the timing has become critical enough to send its message through the subconscious by way of a vivid and memorable dream. Through this method we are presented, in a repetitive manner, with that which we refuse to consciously face, yet can no longer be indefinitely ignored or denied. An analogy would be like being forced to look in a mirror which reflects the true reality at which one must look head-on and finally admit that he/she must now accept its existence and take corresponding action.

This action may be as simple as gaining *acceptance* for something in one's life which she/he was refusing to tolerate or acknowledge. This action may be a push to make some type of decision or choice which the dreamer has been procrastinating in manifesting. There are limitless reasons for the presentation of dream messages. The essential aspect to remember is that they come with weighted significance to positively influence one's life in an encouraging and productive manner through the deliverance of inner guidance, insights, and the revelation of subconsciously hidden life aspects.

What does it mean to dream of cloudy aquarium water?

This dream element would mean that one's spiritual beliefs are clouded. This could refer to conceptual confusion, whereby an individual has mixed together aspects of differing concepts, or it could be pointing to a general confusion resulting from a lack of conceptual clarity. It's even possible that this "cloudiness" represents one's indecision regarding which concepts to accept and believe in. Another clue to the precise meaning of this dream element would be to note what species of fish were within the aquarium. The water's cloudiness could be directly related to the symbology of the fish themselves. For instance, if angelfish were swimming around in the cloudy water it would mean that the individual lacks clarity in understanding the "finer aspects of spiritual truth." If the fish in the tank were platys, it would interpret as meaning a "mental restlessness in regard to being bounded by traditional beliefs when one has a budding desire to expand into the discovery of higher truths." If the aquarium fish were algae-eaters, it would signify a "lack of recognizing one's spiritual blessings or some type of spiritually nourishing aspect in the individual's life." Generally, cloudy water—no matter if it's in an aquarium, freshwater lake, pond, sea, or ocean—means a lack of spiritual conceptual clarity.

What does it mean to have a dream which centers around a bird that doesn't exist in reality?

This dream fragment (the bird) is attempting to draw your attention to the fact that, in reality, you're not exhibiting rational or logical thought patterns. It means that you're thinking illogically or with more "imagined" ideologies than ones which are solidly grounded within reality.

I dreamed that my bedroom became very dark and my husband was standing over in the corner. Intense fear gripped me and I tried to scream, but couldn't. What did this mean?

Whenever a strong, emotional sensation is associated with the appearance of another individual in one's dream, that emotion is a visual presentation of an insight which one has, in the awake state, ignored or refused to acknowledge. In this case, the dream is attempting to display the reality of a need to be more "aware" of your husband's behavior. There is something there that you're missing and need to give more attention to. The dream expression of fear carries great credence and should never be ignored, because it indicates some type of forewarning message. So often when fear is evidenced by our alter-selves within a dreamscape, we have a natural tendency to brush this emotion off upon awakening, because we rationalize that it was so silly. We seem to have an instinctual reaction to consciously deny the potentiality of harm coming from someone close to us, yet oftentimes that is the case. Dreams are wonderful sources of insight which enliven our psychic capabilities, which are frequently dulled or ignored during the waking state.

I'm not an American Indian, so is it okay for me to have a totem animal?

Wait a minute. You made it sound as though totems were unique to the Indian People. Totems are not an ethnic-specific ideology. All of life emits energy influence which affects all other life forms. All people have dreams. All people can have visions. Ergo, all people can have a particular animal present itself to them. We mustn't lose sight of the fact that reality is reality. Reality exists. It exists by and of itself and can affect every other facet of that self, including all people. Reality exists, therefore, it maintains a viable, open, and ready availability to everyone. Just because a certain ethnic group *coined* a concept of reality with a term doesn't equate to that group *owning* it. See? Reality is reality, period. Dreams come to everyone. And visions have been coming to individuals from all ethnic cultures from the beginning of time—case in point being the saints and spiritual mystics throughout history. Visions are an inherent characteristic of the human consciousness which neither requires nor needs ceremony, sacred objects, teacher, nor quest to generate their manifestation. They are generated from within the consciousness and, therefore, cannot be forced. The reality of them is that it's far better to restrain from consciously forcing a vision through fasting or drugs. These causal factors will usually alter a true vision in some manner which is directly associated with one's psychological makeup rather than presenting itself as a true and pure vision of one's *clear* consciousness. There is a definite difference between the two. The former one will be more related to a hallucinogenic visual while the latter, as perceived through the clarity of a clear mind, will be more actual and present itself without surreal facets which only serve to confuse the message. So the totem this correspondent is referring to is valid for him. He saw it and experienced its message in a vision during deep meditation. This alone validates this individual's right to accept and cherish that which came to him.

I dreamed that I was in a café and that I paid for everyone's lunch. Does that mean that I have a "generous" personality?

On the surface I suppose it'd be natural to interpret this dream as meaning generosity, but it has a sub-surface, symbolized intent. The idea this dream is conveying is centered on the "free lunches" element. Normally the dream fragment of a "free lunch" symbolizes an unexpected benefit that presents itself in one's life, or a positive aspect which comes without thought or personal effort applied to its manifestation. But in this particular dreamscape, you are giving everyone in the cafe a free lunch. Taking the analytical process of this dream deeper, we find that this represents *manipulation* because you've not given those diners a "choice" to accept your offer or pay for their own meal (way).

You see? You walked in and actively affected the life of everyone in that diner by immediately taking control. You gave no thought to their individual needs. What if some of those diners needed a meal receipt to claim on their business expense account? Didn't think of that, did you? No, because you gave no thought to the other person's needs or desires, you gave no option for individual choice. And that's the crux of your dream message—you manipulate others through thoughtlessness, by taking away their choices in life. Sometimes generosity has a negative aspect in that, unless it is openly *offered* to an individual *before* the act of giving is manifested, it can be perceived or responded to as being an act of control, manipulation, or interference. Even acts of generosity must be preceded by thoughts of the other individual's individuality and right to choose.

You may think this sounds nitpicky and trite, but it is not. We must keep our minds open to the desires of others before we run out with our hearts full of generosity. I know this to be a viable tenet of spiritual philosophy by learning it through personal experience.

My own example was when I was planning on establishing an outlet for free goods to the public to come and take without any red tape involved or forms to fill out. Anyway, I came across a ramshackle building that had gone up for sale in my area. The price was ridiculously low and I immediately envisioned one side of the building as being this outlet for goods and the other side being a place for a friend of mine to establish her new massage business. I'd mentioned this idea to a different friend who, in turn, mentioned it to my masseuse friend. I heard back that the idea was not received well because I was the one determining where my friend was going to set up her business.

See how complex "giving" can get? What I innocently wanted to do could actually be interpreted as control or manipulation; yet in reality, all I was thinking about was how wonderful it'd be to provide her with a business space and the both of us be located in one building. But when thoughts of generosity come to mind, we must also think of the recipient's personal plans or right to make choices and decisions. When I first heard of her response, I initially thought it was silly because I never harbored any intent to control; but upon deeper introspection, I fully understood the ramifications of my plan. It never materialized because I dropped the entire idea about trying to secure the building after my partner for the goods outlet lost all interest in helping me with it. So, in the long-run, the building wouldn't have been the great idea I'd thought it was. Rule of thumb: When the warmth of generosity fills one's heart, give the recipient a chance for input before acting on impulse. It does seem a shame to have to analyze our impulses of generosity, but the reality of the situation is that we really do need to think our plans through before impulsively putting them into action.

What sort of wisdom does a tree teach?

You seem to think everything in nature is a teacher. Well, that's because every little thing in nature is a teacher, but only if one takes the time to *observe* and *recognize* that wisdom.

You have to spend time with a teacher in order to hear the lessons, observe the example set, and be inspired by the wisdom which naturally emanates from the beingness of same. Your question impels me to ask what experience you've had with trees other than driving past them during the rush-hour journey home from work? A tree. A single tree is a teacher of many types of wisdom. A tree has *perseverance* and *fortitude* to, year after year, endure the manifestations of reality which affect it. It shows *acceptance* for the chilling winter snow and wind by *making adjustments* to the harshness of the climatical change. It *works with* the unavoidable aspects of its surroundings. It *acknowledges* that the changes in life are natural.

A tree *shelters* and *nurtures* others living within its sphere of existence. It *celebrates blessings* such as the rain and sunlight. It *increases its fruitfulness* each year by *multiplying its bounties* of seeds and nuts. Each year it *becomes a stronger entity* through inner growth. It *brings comfort to others* by way of its cool shade on a hot day. It *nourishes and replenishes* the earth each autumn when its leaves fall to ground. I could continue, but I think I've given enough examples of how a tree teaches us the wisdom of right living. Bringing comfort to others, growing and developing more each year, being fruitful, accepting the less desirable elements of life with grace, recognizing and celebrating one's blessings, increasing one's beneficial gifts to others, all clearly exemplify important spiritual lessons we humans can greatly gain from learning and applying to our own lives. The tree—how little credence and substance humans give it. How blind people are to its incredible power to teach us the qualities of experiencing wise living. How silent is its noble character, its beautiful essence, its gentle yet magnificent consciousness.

What does it mean when someone dreams that their car muffler is broken?

It means that someone needs to "muffle" their verbosity, usually their tendency to give unasked-for opinions or their penchant for gossip. Dream symbology is really quite literal in that each element can usually be readily associated with a commonly recognized meaning like that of the muffler. Since a muffler "quiets" loud "noise," this transfers to the "noise from one's mouth" and the caution to quiet that disruptive sound which is an irritation to others who hear it. Perhaps the dreamer is self-possessed and others are weary of hearing about the wonderful qualities or abilities of self.

Maybe the dreamer has a habit of spreading hearsay or continually attempts to indulge others in conversation about others (gossip). It could be that the dreamer is constantly telling others what to do or being too quick to give personal advice. Or perhaps the dreamer is always analyzing others and giving unwanted suggestions for behavioral alterations in others. There could be a multitude of reasons for one's higher self to try to "muffle" one's yakking habit. Self-examination and introspection is needed to pinpoint the precise causal factor. Usually this isn't a dark mystery to solve.

A dream message which cautions one to muffle his or her mouth comes not as a direct chastisement, but rather enters the dream to help the individual improve life conditions, situational aspects, and the quality of personal relationships. It comes to inspire behavioral reflection and introspection which, hopefully, will generate a change for the better. This dream element is attempting to make one recognize the fact that the dreamer's own behavior is what is causing life difficulties in regard to relationships or the perception others have of the dreamer. Frequently, people with big mouths don't even realize how they're sounding to others. This dream facet highlights the focus on "noise"—sound—coming from self and heard by others. Clearly, if that sound requires a muffler, then it's pretty obvious that the dreamer needs to screen his/her thoughts before verbalizing them. The bottom line here is that the dreamer needs to apply thought *before* speaking his/her mind.

In a dream, I saw numbers on the foreheads of all the old people. What did this mean?

In your letter, you also wrote that most of the numerals were the number seven. The number seven means spiritual attainment. This dream fragment is telling you to stop ignoring the elders in your life. It's telling you that they're not as stupid or feeble-minded as you perceive them to be. It's clearly giving you the strong message that you need to learn from the old folks in your life. They have gained immeasurable amounts of knowledge over the years that have blossomed into true experiential wisdom, which you could greatly gain from if you would only recognize the possibility.

My life partner has been recently having repetitive dreams about her being in some type of servant role. Does this mean that she thinks she's being servile in some manner in real life?

Dreams don't normally represent what folks "think" because they're already aware of their awake-state thoughts. Dreams usually present true states of reality which are oftentimes the opposite of what people think they are. I would say that your partner's higher self is telling her that someone in her life is manipulating or controlling her. This doesn't necessarily imply that it's you, but it will be someone close enough to her to be in a position of influence. Perhaps it's some associate at work, a friend, or relative. It could even be religiously related such as a church leader or organization. It could be a social group which operates from some type of cynical or highly opinionated perspective.

Whatever the source, the dream of being a servant represents a real-life situation of psychological manipulation. There is probably the likelihood that your partner is being intimidated enough to withhold personal opinions when with this individual or group. She will perhaps feel somewhat inferior or less strong in their presence and won't be comfortable expressing her own unique individuality while with this person or group.

Intimidation and manipulation creates a servile sense of self. It demeans one's self-confidence and assurance. It makes one feel inferior—as a servant. I suggest you talk to your partner, not only about her dreams, but more importantly, about those individuals and groups she associates with in life. The deeper one looks into relationships and the behavioral facets of them, the clearer one's perspective becomes of the psychological technicalities which are played out between the people involved.

We don't always consciously see the mind games others utilize throughout their lives as a routine manner of acting, but dreamscape fragments can highlight these destructive aberrations and bring them into clear focus for us to look at and understand. It's important for your partner to realize that nobody can manipulate, control, or intimidate her without her consent. That may sound harsh, but it's true. Everyone has individuality. It is that uniqueness which makes us all so special. No one is greater than another, hence no one can lord over another. Everyone's individuality is a beautiful expression of characteristic beingness—the very essence of self. That essence is the who of you.

Differentness represents diversity. Diversity represents the magnificent patchwork of society which celebrates individuality of person and thought. To each her own. To each her own uniqueness and the freedom to express same. It's a fact that uniqueness cannot be intimidated. Think about that. If you truly believe that you're an individual . . . a *unique* individual . . . then you cannot be intimidated by any type of comparison or contrast to the so-called, traditional "norm" which society thinks it identifies as a conformity to its establishment. You are an individual. You are unique. Unique . . . cannot . . . be . . . intimidated. If you truly understand this fact, truly understand it, then you can never be made to feel inferior unless . . . you *allow* it.

I dreamed that my favorite charm was corroded. Can you help me interpret this?

First we need to define what a "charm" represents in dreams. A charm symbolizes a lack of faith or trust. In essence, it means that the individual who possesses such a charm is lacking in self-confidence because he/she requires something touchable to depend on and take courage from. A charm is a psychological crutch. To dream that such a charm is corroded is to be given the message that you don't need to depend on forces outside of self because a corroded charm is a tainted, encrusted, useless object which has no effect upon your own strong beingness. The charm was presented as being corroded in order for the message to convey destructiveness. Not only is the charm destroyed, but the intent of the dream is to inform you that the very *idea* of the charm is destructive to one's self-reliance and sense of self. It indirectly tells you to have the courage to stand on your own two feet and to experience the well of inner strength you inherently have within you. A charm is like someone's "lucky piece." There's no such thing as a "lucky piece" because luck is like positive thinking. It's the *mind* and it's potentiality which can affect positive outcomes, not some physical object. The mind generates energy. Energy moves out from one's beingness. This energy affects everything it comes in contact with. So it's the mind, not a lucky piece or charm which makes things happen. The charm or lucky piece is merely a physical, touchable manifestation of one's own confidence. It's an object to inject one's confidence into, but the actual confidence does not come from the object itself. See the difference? Sometimes people lose faith in self and, therefore, believe they have to have an object to place their belief and confidence in. This object can become such an important part of their life that they feel completely lost if it's misplaced. These people need to realize that it's their own mind, efforts, and talent which manifest their reality, not any kind of physical charm or talisman.

Can a star be one's totem? A star?

A totem is any living essence with a face. Perhaps your star has a face. I'm not being smart-mouthed here, I'm being serious. Your so-called star could actually be a symbolic representation of your *idea* of that which "stars" in your life. What I'm trying to convey is that you may have a special type of animal totem in your life which you don't readily recognize as being such; yet you do recognize a special, beneficial force in your life which you subconsciously transfer by giving the totem's "star" characteristic to a real celestial star. Transference is not uncommon when an individual doesn't consciously recognize a personal totem.

Every time I dream of God, He's a She! What's wrong?

Nothing. Everything's okay. The Trinity consists of two feminine deities. Your higher self isn't bound by conventional, religious dogmas because it only has eyes for the truth of reality. The perceptive reality of those soul eyes are what is received by your subconsciousness through your dreams. This is such a clear and definitive dream that there is absolutely nothing to interpret. There is no symbology at all. It is literal.

In my dreams there's always a shadow behind me. No matter where I am in a dream or what I'm doing, the shadow is there behind me. What's up with this?

Guilt. The shadow represents guilt that needs to be expunged from your conscience. Find a way to forgive yourself because . . . God does.

I know that seeing a halo around people's heads in dreams mean spiritual enlightenment, but what if I see it around my own all the time?

Well then this would symbolize spiritual arrogance, wouldn't it? Yes, because a truly spiritual individual never sees self as being such.

All my decisions seem to be wrong ones. Why don't I have any intuition?

You do; everyone does; the problem is that many people don't recognize it when it comes to them. Intuition is nothing more than random thoughts or physical sensations which suddenly come upon one. Usually one takes note of these but gives them no credence and brushes them off as being odd or inconsequential, therefore, the intuitive insights are not given the prioritized attention they were meant to generate. Let me give you an example of this taken from my own experience. While grocery shopping, I moseyed down an aisle and passed the flour. Intuition said, "better pick some up," but I brushed off the sudden thought and, instead, I told myself that I had plenty at home in the cupboard. Yet while putting the newly purchased groceries away, to my disappointment, I found that I was entirely out of flour. I could kick myself when I realize I should've listened to those little bits of helpful insights that knew the true state of reality better than I did. You probably do the same thing too. I think everyone does. You receive thoughts that could be helpful, but brush them off without giving them credence by acting upon them. Listen more to your thoughts and you'll discover that you do experience intuitive insights. All you have to do is give them the attention they deserve.

Would having a totem animal help raise the level of my self-confidence?

Depending on the type of totem animal, it very well could raise the level of your self-confidence, but then that's not the reason for having a totem. Your reason shows that you're looking at a totem with an eye to obtain a crutch. You need to realize that self-confidence is just what it says it is: *self* confidence—confidence generated from *within* self. And this can only come from you. You need to understand that you are a beautiful, unique individual. You need to fully comprehend that every person walking this earth is a *separate* entity. Every separate entity is different and, different does not mean inferior. Look at the whole of society as being a huge, living crystal with each cut facet being a person. Each facet is an individual, one is you. You are no less important than all the other facets surrounding you. So why do you need more confidence in self? You are, at the very least, equal to the others you see around you. You need to celebrate your wonderful individuality . . . the unique essence that is you and you alone. There is no measuring tape of life by which each person must "measure up"; there is only spiritual goodness to fill our lives with. That is the only criteria for being a good person and a productive individual. Society has developed skewed guidelines for measuring a person's worth. These include social status, level of education, physical characteristics, manner of dress, etc. All of these are trite and inconsequential when weighed against the true reality of personal worth. Don't get caught in society's perceptual silliness. It has no substance when attempting to associate with the real value of an individual.

My neighbor thinks I'm nuts because I told her that my dog's behavior has taught me so much. I bet you don't think I'm nuts. Comment?

You're right, I don't. The incredible unconditional love I receive from my own dogs continues to cause me amazement and deep comfort. That attribute alone proves that our pets exhibit more behavior full of wisdom than humans do. Humans are prejudicial and judgmental. Dogs don't pick and choose who to love by sifting one's beingness of race, creed, social status, or physical characteristics through a judgemental sieve before deciding how they will respond. Dogs live with an acceptance of life (each hour) without having any kind of expectations. They're trusting . . . honest, without false affectations masking their pure emotions which are openly and freely expressed. Oh yes, I absolutely agree with you.

A lot of times my dreams have clocks with hands moving backwards. What does this mean?

The intent of this dreamscape element could be indicating one of two messages. One, that you *need* to "go back" and give corrective attention to something in your past, or two, that you need to *stop* living in the past because that behavior is hindering your advancement. When dream symbols have the potentiality to represent more than one message, only the dreamer can know the precise intent because it will be obvious to him or her. Are you holding a grudge? Are you resentful of a past event or relationship which didn't manifest as expected? Are you living with hate in your heart? Something needs to be resolved by going back and correcting a negative emotion or perspective. That dreamscape clock will not go forward until you do.

More often than not, the animals in my dreams are blue. Isn't this rather strange?

Not really. Blue represents spirituality and, to have the animals in your dreams also be blue means that you need to begin recognizing that there are important lessons you need to learn from the animals in your life. These animals are your teachers and you're not listening to them, nor are you even aware of their potential as teachers. In your awake state, observe these animals more closely. Contemplate their behavior and you'll be pleasantly surprised to realize the wisdom they instill.

I have recurring dreams in which all the people in them are zombies. Can you help me understand why this is happening?

Like the former question about the backwards clock, this dreamscape fragment can have two different meanings. The first one is that you are either consciously or subconsciously manipulating those around you. When this is done, it's as though you create people with no individuality to be themselves, but rather how you want them to be—all alike, without personal opinion or individuality. The second reason for this symbology is that your personal perception of people's intellect as a whole is one of "herd mentality" which means that they "mindlessly" follow popular opinion regardless of their own unique ideologies. They are fearful to openly express a differing perspective or attitude. Everyone is emotionally and intellectually void. Now remember, the elements of dreams most frequently symbolize that which is hidden from the individual's consciousness or intentionally shoved into one's subconsciousness.

In this case if, in the awake state, you *know* you perceive people as being mindless, therefore, a dream symbol isn't necessary to tell you this, is it? This then leaves the remaining intent of bringing to the forefront of your consciousness your negative element of being a manipulative person. It's not unusual for an individual to be consciousnessly unaware that he/she has a tendency to exhibit habitual behavior which is controlling and manipulative. This is why this specific type of dream fragment manifests—for the purpose of visually presenting the dreamer with images of this behavior. Frequently intentions are good, but the actualization of them doesn't quite make an exact alignment with those innocent objectives and can, in the end, result in deeds which control rather than aid. This then is not saying that you're some bad guy who goes around intentionally making everyone do as you say. No, this doesn't necessarily mean that. What this zombie element is telling you is to "look" closer at your own behavior, to more closely observe how that behavior affects those around you, how that behavior is received and responded to. Is it accepted with the same attitude it was given? How are people reacting to your behavior? Not every manipulative person is aware of that behavior.

I want to relocate to a geographical region which will be safe for the future so before I fall asleep, I mentally concentrate on an intention for receiving this insight. The dreams that ensue will depict an outline of the U.S., but the interior is blank. What's going on here?

Your higher self is attempting to tell you that the information you seek through symbology will instead come through your awake state. Where you live (move to) is a choice which must be made by the conscious mind. All associated life elements must be properly analyzed and correspondingly factored in. To expect a dream to circumvent this important process is to ignore your responsibility to make an intellectual decision. This dream fragment is telling you that you need to shoulder that responsibility rather than opting to seek a quick way to avoid expending personal effort toward that goal. Granted, it would be so simple if we could all just dream our life solutions and answers to the daily problems and dilemmas, but it doesn't work that way. More times than not, the resulting dream will end up telling you this very thing. In this case, the blank interior of the U.S. is intending to urge you to "think for self." It is not giving you any indication of a specific region. It's not pinpointing nor highlighting a particular area on the map. It's entirely blank. It is saying that the answer you seek is *within you* already; go within.

Lately, every time I have dreams of my workplace, I'm watching a safety film. Isn't this rather odd? Repetitive?

Yes, it's certainly repetitive, but it's not odd. This dream aspect is attempting to tell you that you need to be more aware at work because there exists some element which has the potentiality to be dangerous or harmful to you. Perhaps this is a physical condition or it could be referring to an associative relationship with a co-worker or management. Review your workdays to see if you can pinpoint some activity, tendency, situation, or behavior which could ultimately lead to an unproductive, unsafe, or damaging result. A safety film evidencing in a dream will always come as an attempt to caution or warn the dreamer to be more aware.

Generally, in life, what wisdom can horseflies possibly teach us?

They're irritating little buggers, aren't they? And what are we to do with so many of life's little irritations? Well, we can put ourselves in a state of constant frustration by continually swatting at them and cussing all the way to a stress-related heart attack, or we can *accept* them with *tolerance* and continue along our way. We have a choice as to which way we respond with our behavior. A horsefly represents acceptance and tolerance of others. In my dream book, the horsefly symbolizes "biting remarks" because this type of verbal responsive behavior is directly due to intolerance and a lack of acceptance. For someone to feel the need to "snap" at others with cruel or unkind comments, means that individual needs to gain the wisdom which acceptance and tolerance instills.

Why do people react to common sense as though it was some esoteric insight?

Recent books which have become highly popular are nothing more than common sense that you'd think these folks already had. Comment? I make a point to not publicly comment on books other than my own because people have a tendency to interpret my opinion as fact and that perspective is not a correct one to have. However, on this point, I do agree. There have been a few recent books that the general public has appeared to be in awe over when, in actuality, their content was nothing more than common sense that you'd think the readers already had. I agree that this phenomena is a confoundment to those who read the last page of the book and were left with a puzzlement and said, "so?"

For those individuals who already had common sense and a normal measure of attained wisdom, these types of books create a sense of discouragement in regard to the intellectual level of society. If common sense is generally perceived as high, esoteric insight, what does that say about the intellectual status of the populace as a whole? It depicts a worrisome state of affairs when people think common sense is the same as high wisdom. I read one of these quite awhile ago and, when I was finished, I felt like the content held nothing more esoteric than if it had been a book explaining how to turn a water faucet on.

Months later, when the book became the talk of the town—every town—it was depressing to me to realize how desperate people were. I had a difficult time observing their awe-filled responses to something that was nothing more than plain and simple common sense. You also saw this happening and it confounded you, too.

I can't give you a definitive explanation for it other than what I've observed of society. I see lazy people who don't want to expend personal energy to work their way toward individual development. I see mental apathy caused by a lack of desire to personally analyze information and form individualized perceptions and firm up conceptual beliefs. I see a strong desire for others to provide the answers and tell them what to believe. I see people elevating simple common sense to the level of deified utterances because they have become so filled with desperation they're blindly reaching for anything they think is new without even taking a good look at the reality of what it really is. Society has de-evolved to such a level that it hears common sense called "enlightenment" or "insight" and it believes it. Wisdom is having a discerning mind which quickly and accurately recognizes the reality of this and understands what true inspiration and enlightenment is when they're encountered.

What does it mean when all the cats I dream about are extremely overweight?

Fat cats. You dream of "fat cats." A fat cat symbolizes an individual possessing a multitude of resources. I know that, normally, when one hears the expression, "fat cat," he or she immediately thinks of someone with deep pockets—a rich person—but the dream fragment goes beyond the common, awake-state interpretation. A dream fat cat will represent an individual who has the capability and wherewithal to readily access a multitude of resources which carry a wide range of potentiality. This dream facet displays the presence of someone (in this case, many people) in your life who could be valuable resources for you if you'd only recognize this potential in them. This dream element is literally telling you that you are surrounded by opportunities.

What does it mean when, in dreams, the photographs I take come back all black with nothing on them?

It means that you're allowing your past to "darken" your present. It is telling you to stop "holding on" to negative, residual emotions which are hampering your ability to perceive the here and now with unbiased clarity. Some event in your past is being allowed to tether you to it through voluntary resentment, anger, jealousy, envy, or other negative emotions. You need to let this go because it's clouding and darkening your current ability to perceive and react to life with acceptance and tolerance, which can only be maintained through intellectual and emotional neutrality, that is to say, an intellectual and psychological state which is unfettered by negatively affecting attitudes. It is as though, quite literally, you're allowing something in your past to completely obliterate and negate your present. Something in your past is so completely affecting your present that it's making your current life meaningless—emotionally blank. This dream element is telling you to resolve this destructive past event so that you can once again begin to experience life with fullness and gain the depth of appreciation and clarity this brings with each passing day.

Why do all the shade trees in my dreams have no leaves?

Well, we know it's not because it's winter, because your letter also stated that these dreams also represent the hottest part of summertime. So then, since shade trees symbolize respite, this dream element is an advisement for you to stop denying yourself a rest period. You're working too hard. Taking time off for a bit of relaxation is more beneficial to continued productivity than keeping your nose to the grindstone and building up internal stress and pressure. Everyone needs a break now and then. A respite is not only good for the physical body and mind, it's also wonderfully refreshing for the soul. Your summertime shade trees are leafless because you choose to make them so. They cannot give refreshment and relief from the blazing heat of the sun if you continue to voluntarily omit them from your awake state by refusing to take that much-needed rest. Why don't you test this theory? Take that break and see if those dreamscape trees don't suddenly give the shade you've been seeking. *Note: I heard back from this work-driven gentleman two months after he wrote me with the above question. He took the challenge. He purposely took a break. His trees had leaves. Wasn't it interesting what wisdom those trees had to share with him?*

It amazes me to see so many people ignoring their intuitive moments. Why do they do this?

Generally, I don't think it's done on a voluntary basis. I think people, for the most part, aren't *aware* of these intuitive insights when they manifest. They don't recognize them for the boon they are and, therefore, don't proceed to give them attention. It's an undeniable fact that hundreds of thoughts continually flow through our minds each day. Only a small percentage of these are snared and examined for further consideration. The intuitive ones are oftentimes so subtle that the consciousness doesn't give them any more credence than taking subliminal note of them while letting them pass through. So many times people shake their heads at these random thoughts, but consider the lucky woman who listened when the thought came to mind to take another way home from work and she responded by doing so, only to later learn that a fatal accident had occurred along her normal route that day.

What does it mean in a dream when a train goes past you and all the cars are cabooses?

A caboose symbolizes some type of finalization, the end of something. In this dreamscape, when every one of the cars are a caboose, the message is a strong one which attempts to get through to your consciousness through repetition. You are being dense about some aspect in your life which has been concluded some time ago. You're not letting it go. You're trying to hold on to something you need to leave in the past. Caboose after caboose after an entire line of cabooses says: "End, end, end. For heaven's sake, let it go and get on with your life!"

What does a blank calling card symbolize in a dream?

This dream fragment indicates one's outward presentation to the public. In other words, false affectations which comprise one's mask. A blank calling card defines this message with greater intensity by way of visually exposing that what the card may have said is meaningless—blank. The key to this dream element is to note *who* presented the card. Was it someone else presenting it to you or was it you handing it over to someone else?

In several of my dreams I was wearing false eyelashes. I'm a man, so does this mean that I have excessive feminine traits?

No, not at all. False eyelashes mean misplaced confidence in one's belief that his or her attitudes and opinions are remaining private. So having false eyelashes means that one is trying to hide true perspectives, thoughts, or real character attributes from the public, but it's not working. People are seeing right through the facade.

What does it mean in dreams when an adult is reading a book and that book is a fairy tale?

It means that the individual in the dreamscape is absorbing higher enlightenment. A dream fragment of a fairy tale represents "hidden lessons" in life.

In my dream, a cannon was rolling out of control down a hill toward me. I can't figure what this means.

Yes you can, if you just think a bit more on it. What would another term for an out of control cannon be? A "loose cannon." And dream's presentation of a loose cannon symbolizes unpredictability, irresponsibility, or untrustworthiness. In life, this term "loose cannon" has come to commonly mean an unpredictable individual, one who could cause trouble or have the capability of shoving a wrench into the gears of another's plans. In your dream this cannon was rolling out of control down a hill toward you. This clearly indicates that someone in your life is on the verge of becoming this loose cannon. This dreamscape fragment is a direct forewarning.

What does it mean in a dream when I can't get my headlights out of low beam?

Low headlight beams symbolize a need for more light on a subject; greater perspective is required for an accurate view or conceptual formulation. Since you couldn't get these lights out of low beam this dream fragment is telling you that you are subconsciously *preventing* more light to be shed on a subject. This then means that you're either being stubbornly opinionated and *closed-minded* about something or else you're *fearful* of what you may discover by shedding more light on something. This dream element is telling you to stop preventing yourself from gaining greater insight and understanding; to stop being fearful of the truth.

I dreamed that, in my home, I had a beautiful statue of an angel, but it was made of pumice stone. Isn't that sort of unusual? I couldn't understand what this meant.

This one's easy. You're going to think so too in a minute. An angel represents spiritual messages, concepts, or qualities. Pumice symbolizes something in one's life which needs to be smoothed out. Put them together. Put them together and they end up indicating a spiritual aspect in your life which is too rough or rigid and needs to be smoothed or rounded out. Only you can pinpoint what this specific aspect is. Perhaps you're not quite behaving in alignment with your beliefs. Maybe your beliefs are far too "sharp" and are sometimes "cutting" while expressing them to others. Anyway, you get the drift. Soften the facets of your spirituality because, in some damaging way, they're not only harming self, they're negatively affecting those around you.

Why do intuitive thoughts of inspiration come when there's no possible way to manifest them?

Because you're in expectation. You're assuming that the time frame for them is now when, in actuality, they may be intuitive *foresight*—meant for a future time in your life. Many times the consciousness exposes insightful intuitiveness which reveals situational events of one's future. In essence, this serves to assist in guiding our footfalls along our destined path. When one becomes cognizant of certain relationships, occupations, events, or situations which are solid elements of his/her future, the present can be more accurately guided toward those actualities down the road. These insightful intuitive messages come as an *extended* peek into the future and lay out a panoramic view of same for us. This type of dream symbol is a true blessing.

Whenever I'm in a dreamscape church, all the stained-glass windows are always what are called rose windows. How come?

A rose window symbolizes a perspective derived from *multiple* associated aspects. *Multiple* is the key word here because, throughout early religious history, the rose symbolized the Mother Goddess and later, the Virgin Mary. In medieval times the rose was believed to represent Mary's feminine doorway through which Jesus was birthed. The rose window in early churches were generally set in a west wall where the sun set and where the Mother Goddess of that mysterious directional land ruled. This rose window was a medallion representing the many-faceted, divine aspects of the

Mother Goddess. The rose and the rose window are symbols of the Mother Goddess and the Virgin Mary. In many churches today, rose windows will include a representation of Mary within them. In this dreamscape, since all the windows of the churches are rose windows, this indicates an advisement for you to open self up to the feminine aspect of your current spiritual belief system. This symbol is a personal revelation through which the rose window speaks from the consciousness of the Divine Mother directly to you. It says, "I exist. I exist for you. See how the splendor of my love for you blazes through your heart. Acknowledge me."

Whenever I dream of my love and myself, we're Romeo and Juliet. Isn't that romantic?

The romance of Romeo and Juliet was a *tragic* affair. You also confided in me that your "love" was not your wife. Doesn't that say something? Isn't this dream element a powerful message? You're only seeing what you want to see. Yes, *Romeo and Juliet* was a romance, but it certainly didn't end happily. It ended in death for both.

I often dream that I'm in a doctor's office, but every time I do, I'm there getting an enema. Why is this?

This is because you're ignoring the fact that you need to shed the superficial and extraneous aspects in your life. This dream element points out that you're placing too much emphasis and importance on insubstantial life facets, maybe the materialistic side. You need to get rid of these superficial perspectives and begin to focus on what's really important in your life. Your priorities are skewed. This "enema" is not intended to imply a physiological condition, but rather a psychological or spiritual facet.

What does it mean in a dream when the word "Chernobyl" is displayed in neon lights?

Chernobyl symbolizes the dangers of having too little knowledge on a subject. Having this word come to you in flashing, neon lights is literally "flashing right before your very eyes" the message that you perceive yourself knowledgeable about a certain subject matter but, in actuality, you are far from it. This symbol is telling you that you are treading dangerous ground because of your "little bit" of knowledge which you think is so great. Now this "knowledge" may be referring to any number of subject matters in your life. Perhaps it has to do with a relationship, the workplace, philosophical ideologies, spiritual concepts or any number of other matters. The point is that only you will know what this is referencing because only you *think* you have this subject covered.

Does seeing an altar with statues of a famous, living personality on it in dreams mean that her spirit is worthy of worship?

This dream fragment is one of those containing duality. Deciding which end of the polarity is being presented specifically for you can only be accurately determined by self—how you're thinking about this individual. This altar with a recognizable statue can intend to caution *against* raising someone up to that level of adoration, or it could be *revealing* that individual's true spiritual state of beingness. Only you can determine which this is by observing other surrounding dream elements associated with this altar.

I dreamed I had a mascot. The mascot was a waif. How can that be?

A waif symbolizes a victim of circumstance, those less fortunate. And since you also detailed your empathy for the homeless and your volunteer works, I'd say that this "waif" is a representation of your spiritually generated corporeal work in life. This mascot has attached itself to you as a companionable personality serving to encourage your continued efforts, to act as a perennial impetus to keep up the good work. I don't mean to imply that this waif is an actual entity. I want that to be clear. The waif is a "symbol" only—the unseen mascot of your compassion and expression of same.

In my dream, a friend of mine threw a fit because we didn't have a yule log for our Christmas gathering. What does this mean?

It means that your friend is far too rigid with his spiritual beliefs. He's confining them within the bounds of tradition rather than allowing them to breathe and expand with the breath of their living reality. He believes that by the omission of the traditional yule log, the Christmas celebration was incomplete and, therefore, almost made null and void because of it.

Why did I dream that my father's den was full of animal trophies on the walls? He wouldn't think of hunting.

This is a dreamscape fragment which reveals a hidden characteristic about another. The animal trophies, remember, are *symbolic*. An animal trophy symbolizes false power or a lack of courage. Now let's look at the associative symbol of a "hunter." A hunter represents an individual who is "searching" for something. Blending these two together, we come up with someone possessing a lack of courage and is also searching for something. Perhaps this "something" the individual is searching for is courage. Many times the dream symbology of the hunter is associated with a search for identity which is falsely gained through the medium of being the "big, powerful hunter" with the "power" coming from the crutch of the gun. Some dream symbology interpreters will even go as far as claiming that the hunter subconsciously perceives his gun as an extension of his manhood. We don't need to take this woman's dream that far, but I would personally interpret her dream as meaning her father lacks self-confidence and has been successful in hiding it.

Whenever I dream of going to the doctor, I'm always there for hypochondria. I'm not a hypochondriac in real life so why am I in these dreams?

Again, as stated in the former response, dream fragments are symbols, not representations of reality. I'm sure you're not a hypochondriac in real life, but in dreams this condition symbolizes an individual who has a tendency to use psychological ploys to gain the sympathy and/or attention of others. Your higher self *knows* self. Your higher self cannot be fooled. It uses dream symbols to provide clear visuals for the individual to look at and identify—to recognize and admit to. This "hypochondriac" is a representation of how you, either subconsciously or knowingly, tend to manipulate others through psychological mechanizations employed to bend them to your will or create a central focus on self.

My friend has rabbits in real life. I dreamed that all her hutches were broken to pieces. What does this mean?

Rabbit hutches symbolize a warning against confining or hiding one's more innocent qualities for fear of ridicule. This means an inferiority complex or lack of self-confidence. To dream that these hutches were broken in pieces is not the negative interpretation it would appear to be. This is a clear, positive sign that your friend is gaining a greater measure of self-confidence and identity, that she's becoming more and more comfortable with her identity and its beautiful uniqueness. Some dream fragments, on the surface, can appear to be a destructive element, but upon closer examination, prove to be just the opposite.

I dreamed I was in a sun-lit, mountain meadow full of blossomed orchids.

Orchids don't grow in high, mountain meadows so how do I interpret this inconsistency? Mmmm, I need to expand further on my published symbology of the "orchid" with this one, because I did my dream symbology book with the "general" public in mind. For a woman, the dream presentation of an orchid most often represents "feminine sexuality." In this specific dream you were in a meadow full of *blossoming* orchids growing in wild profusion. In line with the rest of the confidential information you shared with me in your letter, this dream clearly indicates your recently developed attitude toward your own sexuality and your beautiful acceptance of the who of you. Like the rose, the orchid often symbolizes feminine genitalia and is often indicative of a direct associative message regarding the individual's conscious acceptance or rejection of her own sexual perception of self and/or her awake-state sexual tendencies. Your particular dream indicates that you accept who you are and are totally comfortable with your pure beingness. You are filled with joy over your femaleness and can now openly celebrate your true self. Congratulations.

Midgets populate my dreams. I'm continually surrounded by them. I'm the biggest person around. Why?

Look at your statement. The way you worded it reveals your answer. In life you perceive self as being the "biggest person around." How more clear do you expect this message to be? Midgets symbolize a caution to never—ever—correlate power or knowledge with size. Larger never means more or greater. Conversely, smaller never means lesser or insignificant. If you accept this interpretation, you'll recognize that your behavior has been one of arrogance and perhaps manipulation.

Lately, in dreams, being some type of investigator seems to be my singular occupation. Why?

Probably because lately, you've been so wrapped up in an intensive spiritual search. You did mention that in your letter. It stands to reason that it'd be logical for your dream occupation to reflect the "work" you're involved in during the awake-state. I'm surprised you've not dreamed that you were Sherlock Holmes by the sound of your search's intensity.

Does wisdom come from knowledge—the gaining of it? What is knowledge?

Knowledge is nothing more than information. Knowledge is gained from extensive reading, studying, research, and listening. Where is the wisdom in that? Oh no, wisdom comes from the proper *application* of that gained knowledge through experiential behavior. I've seen incredibly knowledgeable intellectuals who didn't possess a half-ounce of wisdom. I've observed scientists who didn't have the wisdom to make the associative relationships between their rigid theorems. I've known hunters who knew all there was to know about hunting and outdoor survival, yet didn't have the wisdom to respect innocent life by recognizing the sacredness of the interrelated threads which catch all of life within the totality of the vibrating great Web of Life. I've seen physicists who can talk circles around the average individual yet can't bring themselves to tolerate a female peer. There are spiritual teachers whose hearts are full of greed. I could go on and on with solid examples of how knowledge does not equate with wisdom. One is easily gained, the other is earned through experience. One is passive, while the other is active. One is neutral, while the other is positive. One is technical, while the other is spiritual in nature. One can advance society, while the other uplifts it.

Why does Darth Vader lurk in the shadows of my dreams?

He lurks there because this character symbol indicates an individual who is misusing spirituality by focusing on negative purposes for its utilization. Simply put, Darth Vader means that you are in possession of spiritual talents which you choose to use in negative or harmful ways. It means that the dark side of spirituality is attracting your interests. Get smart. Get some real wisdom. That's what this dream fragment is trying to tell you.

Last night I had a really odd dream. I dreamed that Charles Darwin was jumping up and down and waving his arms shouting, "No, no!" as he was giving a lecture in an auditorium. What did this mean?

Well, clearly the man was desperately trying to get the audience's attention. His words give an unequivocable message, don't they? The man is famous for the Darwinian Theory of Evolution. Now you see him shouting, "No, no!" What could he be saying no about?

It would be logical to associate his exclamations to his theory. Have you recently been pondering the theory of evolution? Here's your answer then. But you knew that, didn't you? You just wanted it verified. And that's okay, but you really should trust your own instincts.

Every dream I have of my boyfriend coming over to my house for dinner, I'm using a pressure cooker. I don't even own one in real life. What's up with this?

Isn't it obvious what's up with this? Clearly the relationship you have with this individual is extremely stressful. A pressure cooker symbolizes an extremely stressful situation, relationship, or element in one's life. This relationship is full of pressure which is about to explode. This dreamscape element is a warning. It comes as a warning.

In real life I play the piano. In my dreams the metronome is always going too slow. How do I make it go faster?

That's just the point. You want life to go faster when you need to slow down. There is always a specific reason for this message. Slow down your pace in life. You think too fast. Or you talk too fast. You expect goals to be reached quickly, far before they reach their full development. Time. Time listens to no one. Time just is. Let it exist. Let it present what it will as reality was meant to advance and fulfill itself. Stop "forcing" life. This dream element also indicates that you're not "accepting" life as it unfolds, that you have a tendency to "push" for actualities and resolutions. This describes impatience. It defines intolerance for proper timing, which causes frustration and irritability, stress and self-generated pressure on self. Is that the way you truly want to live life? Your dream is warning you to accept life as it comes and slow down. Maybe it foresees a dangerous physiological condition developing if you don't. Dreams do this, you know. The insightful foresight of one's higher self talks to us through dreams and intuitive thoughts. Pay attention to them. You just may avoid a heart-attack or some other stress generated disease. Your higher self wants you to live.

I dreamed that the book, **Living Is Forever,** *came true and one of the main leaders of the survivors was a female visionary. Could this be a premonition?*

Sure it could. Personally, I believe J. Edwin Carter was inspired by high spiritual forces when he wrote the book. Sometimes dreams *verify* the truth to aspects in real life. They come to emphasize and underscore the accuracy of the subliminal thoughts or questioning ideas we receive in life. There are types of dreams that are reinforcing mechanisms for our conscious thoughts. This is one of them.

Why are all the eggs in my dream refrigerator colored Easter eggs? I don't get this.

Easter eggs symbolize "colored" or decorated perceptions. You have this dream element because your higher self is attempting to tell you that you need to stop "embellishing" or "coloring" your perceptions.

You're adding to or altering that which you see and observe in life. You're skewing things to make a self-created reality, one which pleases you more than *what is*. And this behavior indicates a lack of acceptance. You need to gain a greater measure of acceptance and tolerance for life. Having acceptance doesn't mean that you necessarily have to like those aspects you don't want to face or acknowledge, it just means that you've gained a tolerance for them by understanding that they're going to exist no matter what you do.

What does an earache represent in a dream?

An earache represents the act or habit of listening to too much verbiage that is extraneous or insignificant. It's as though this message is telling you that everything you give listening attention to is no more than "noise which hurts" the mind (ear). This dream element indicates a lack of perceptual and intellectual discrimination. It means that you take in all you hear without qualifying it.

The full moon in my latest dream was a clear lunar eclipse. What did this represent?

This represented an awareness of true existential reality which has been temporarily forgotten. What I'm saying is that you inherently know the truths to spiritual reality, but sometimes they become elusive for you. The full moon stands for deep wisdom and high spiritual knowledge. An eclipse of it means a lapse in conscious awareness or memory of this wisdom and knowledge. The total symbology of the full moon symbolizes feminine wisdom and is directly associated to the Mother Goddess of Wisdom. In my dream symbology book I gave the "general" interpretation of this dream fragment rather than expanding it further into a gender-specific interpretation. So in respect to your specific dream, this feminine aspect would apply to mean that you're forgetting what your higher self knows—to celebrate the feminine aspect of spiritual reality and remember that the Mother Deity exists.

Why is my workplace always faded in dreams when every other location is sharp and clear?

This is because your higher self, through the medium of dream elements, is foretelling of the future eventuality of changing jobs. Your workplace is presented in "fade-out" because it is in the process of fading out. You may not be consciously aware of the potentiality for this right now, but as time passes, events will lead you into another occupation or outlet for the expression of your current skill.

Why do my dreams show my boyfriend with fangs instead of normal teeth?

This happens because fangs indicate vicious or cutting speech. Your higher self may be attempting to inform you that this individual is not talking about you in the manner you think he is. It may be telling you that you need to give more attention to how he talks, perhaps give it greater attention rather than ignoring it. For some reason, this is important for you; otherwise the dream aspect wouldn't have presented itself.

I dreamed that my alter-ego was a mole. Could this represent my totem?

Probably not. I'm more inclined to think this is a dream symbol representing your lack of self-confidence. A mole indicates a lack of communication or a fear of reality. Having a fear of reality means that you hold yourself in low esteem and don't have self-reliance or the confidence that attends it. You feel cowered by life or those you come in contact with when, in reality, you need to love yourself and stand tall beside others. If this mole was your totem, that's exactly what its energy would influence you to do.

In my dream I developed ringworm. What's that supposed to mean?

That's supposed to mean that you're far too impulsive in life. That means you don't watch where you're stepping, due to a tendency to rush into things before taking the valuable time to apply analytical thought.

On my dream dresser, there is always a photograph of my girlfriend, but instead of a modern day, color photograph, it's a sepia daguerreotype. Can you explain why this is?

This dreamscape element is revealing a past-life association with this woman. You have known her before and have experienced a close relationship with her. This is not to assume nor claim that she and you were lovers as now, but it does mean to convey some type of close association in the past.

Is there a way to stop intuitiveness or spontaneous mental visuals from coming to mind?

This person's question was inspired by a frustration of having visual insights without the attending knowledge which clarifies their meanings. I admit that's incredibly irritating, but clarity usually comes with the passing of time. Nobody should want to put up a solid barrier to intuitiveness or spontaneous insight because they're a natural and inherent aspect of our beingness. They are as blessings which heighten awareness and hone personal perception. They serve to sharpen our ability to make correct decisions and choices in life. They're a part of our higher sensibilities of spirit. They're our connection to the delicate vibrations felt from reality's Web of Life.

How come all my intuitiveness comes from dreams and not when I'm awake?

It sounds to me as though this may be happening because you might not *trust* your awake-state insights and perceptions. You may not want to recognize or accept the responsibility for them. In the dream time, you can have a sense of being once removed from that responsibility as though these insights were coming from somewhere "without" self. Yet, in reality, they come from your own subconscious—your own inner knowing.

Do human emotions affect nature?

Every vibration emanating from every life form affects every other life form. All of life is sensitive. All of life is perceptive and responsive to receptivity. Have you ever noticed how well house plants do, how well they grow and thrive in a serene or happy household? How sickly they can become in an angry or despondent household? Love raises vibrations. Love creates an incredible energy which causes life to thrive—to *want* to thrive. Love is a vibration. When that vibration courses along the living threads of the Web of Life, every cell benefits.

Deep in a forest, green and lush,
lies a fragile web off the
well-worn trail . . . vibrating.

Deep in a forest, sparkling with
dew, lies the secret of life hidden
from view . . . singing.